THIS BOOK BELONGS TO
The Library of

....

....

COPYRIGHT 2024

The content contained within this book may not be reproduced, duplicated, or transmitted without direct written permission from the author or the publisher. Under no circumstances will any blame or legal responsibility be held against the publisher, or author, for any damages, reparation, or monetary loss due to the information contained within this book. Either directly or indirectly.

Legal Notice:
This book is copyright protected. This book is only for personal use. You cannot amend, distribute, sell, use, quote, or paraphrase any part, or the content within this book, without the consent of the author or publisher.

Disclaimer Notice:
Please note the information contained within this document is for educational and entertainment purposes only. All effort has been executed to present accurate, up-to-date, and reliable, complete information. No warranties of any kind are declared or implied. Readers acknowledge that the author is not engaging in the rendering of legal, financial, medical, or professional advice. The content within this book has been derived from various sources. Please consult a licensed professional before attempting any techniques outlined in this book. By reading this document, the reader agrees that under no circumstances is the author responsible for any losses, direct or indirect, which are incurred as a result of the use of the information contained within this document, including, but not limited to — errors, omissions, or inaccuracies.

Thank you for Purchasing my book and taking the time to read it from front to back. I am always grateful when a reader chooses my work and I hope you enjoyed it!

With the vast selection available online, I am touched that you chose to be purchasing my work and take valuable time out of your life to read it. My hope is that you feel you made the right decision.

I very much would like to know what you thought of the book. Please take the time to write an honest and informative review on Amazon.com. Your experience and opinions will be of great benefit to me and those readers looking to make an informed choice.

With much thanks.

Table of Contents

INTRODUCTION	5
CHAPTER 1 WHAT IS CRYPTOCURRENCY?	11
CHAPTER 2 HOW DO I GET CRYPTO?	28
CHAPTER 3 HOW MANY CRYPTOCURRENCIES ARE THERE?	43
CHAPTER 4 ARE CRYPTOCURRENCIES LEGAL?	59
CHAPTER 5 HOW DO I PROTECT MYSELF FROM SCAMMERS?	70
CHAPTER 6 ARE CRYPTOCURRENCIES A GOOD INVESTMENT?	86
CHAPTER 7 TEN IMPORTANT CRYPTOCURRENCIES OTHER THAN BITCOIN BY MARKET CAPITALIZATION	94
CONCLUSION	104

Introduction

It is not a hidden secret for most movie lovers how Hollywood script writers have become notoriously accurate in predicting new science and technology over the last few decades. While movies will always remain a source of entertainment for viewers, these futuristic films set in times ahead have opened our eyes to the limitless possibilities in the future. Some of these movies that have easily blown the minds of viewers include "The Fifth Element (1997)," "Minority Report (2002)," "I, Robot (2004)," and many more.

Apart from being richly entertaining, they are characterized mainly by a bold display of high-end technologies such as flying cars and humanoid robots. But, more importantly, these movies tend to point to a future that sees the world become more connected through shared interests and even currency. Decades ago, the idea that the world would share a currency would have been unfathomable due to several mitigating factors, including language, culture, religion, and contrasting government policies.

Also making things more complicated is the fact that there are currently 164 official national currencies that their governments fiercely back. Still, thanks to the internet and sheer ingenuity, the last decade has seen the emergence of cryptocurrency as a significant force in world economics.

How Did Cryptocurrency Become So Popular?

Technology continues to be a significant game-changer in almost every sphere of our lives — it has changed the way we think, work, communicate, shop, and even pay for goods. With the world embracing cashless transactions and payments, the need for an alternative to traditional currencies became more critical.

In January 2009, the first digital currency known as bitcoin was created by someone or a group of people who continue to be identified by the pseudonym Satoshi Nakamoto. Interestingly, despite the subsequent meteoric rise of bitcoin over the last decade, nobody knows the true identity of those who created this cryptocurrency.

While bitcoin was created in 2009, its paper trail can be traced back a couple of months to the aftermath of the 2008 financial crisis that tore through the world's economic systems. Consequently, many people suffered huge financial losses, which understandably generated a lot of anger directed towards banks and governments.

Amidst all the anger and frustration, one obvious thing was that people had become disillusioned with the arrangement of having to trust banks and governments with their hard-earned money. Without mincing words, people wanted more control of their money, and the introduction of Bitcoin gave them that power. Bitcoin was specifically created to give people the ability to control their money without government or financial institutions like banks, making it the first-ever peer-to-peer currency.

In essence, cryptocurrency gives people the complete freedom to do whatever they desire with their money at any time and with anyone around the world. The only restrictions here are those that an individual puts up for their convenience. More importantly, these transactions can be carried out while still ensuring your anonymity. In other words, your transactions are well secured and kept private, leaving you with the power to choose what you decide to let people know about what you are doing with your money.

In a nutshell, crypto has helped people break free from the various constraints placed on their money by the banks and government policies. Initially, the acceptance of crypto was mainly championed by the younger generation. And it has become commonplace for millennials and generation Z not to have traditional bank accounts. Unsurprisingly, the last few years have seen the use of digital currencies gain wider acceptance across age and border.

While financial freedom has been a significant selling point for cryptocurrency, there are several other reasons why it has gained massive popularity amongst its supporters. These include:

- Most of the users of cryptocurrencies such as Bitcoin see it as the "money of the future" and scramble to purchase as much as possible because they believe it will be more valuable in the coming years.
- In addition, some of the supporters enjoy the fact that crypto removes central banks from the money supply chain, thereby eliminating the possibility of reducing their money through inflation that these banks trigger.
- Other supporters like the blockchain technology behind cryptocurrency because it is a decentralized processing and recording system that has proven to be more secure than the traditional payment systems.

Cryptocurrencies such as Bitcoin also guarantee lower transaction fees when compared to traditional online payment mechanisms. Also, its potential for growth and appreciation is another appealing factor for many of its users.

Since its introduction in 2009, Bitcoin has gained massive followership, but it is still not seen as a legal tender by several countries worldwide. However, its wide acceptance by people has helped inspire the introduction of several other cryptocurrencies, collectively described as altcoins.

According to CoinMarketCap.com, a market research website, there are over 6,700 cryptocurrencies currently being traded publicly. Some of these cryptocurrencies include Ethereum, Binance Coin, Tether, Cardano, Polkadot, XRP, Uniswap, Litecoin, Stellar, Dogecoin, and many more.

No Need to be Afraid

While Bitcoin and other digital currencies continue to grow in popularity with every passing day, research has shown that there is still so much skepticism surrounding it. This is due to many people not fully understanding cryptocurrency. Unlike traditional currencies that we grew up knowing and are even taught extensively in school, there is still relatively little information about cryptocurrency. Moreover, despite the popularity gained by Bitcoin over the last decade, the cryptocurrency space is still very much in its developmental phase. So it can be a bit scary or confusing for newcomers who are not equipped with adequate information.

Just like everything digital, the cryptocurrency space is vast and rapidly growing. Earlier I mentioned how there are currently 164 official national currencies. When you compare that to the thousands of digital currencies being traded publicly, it is easy to see why it could confuse beginners. Yet, new cryptocurrencies are developed faster than you can come to grasp with the ones available.

Understandably, there is the question of where to invest and which cryptocurrencies to put your money into for many beginners. However, before you invest any of your money, you must understand cryptocurrency exchanges. Today, there are over 500 platforms that provide a means to buy and sell digital currencies, and you should talk to an experienced investor before diving in.

Apart from discussing the benefits of investing in cryptocurrency and how to get started in the crypto market, this book will open your eyes to other challenges you may face as a beginner and how to overcome them. These include:

- How to protect yourself from online theft or hackers
- How to identify some of the best companies to invest your money. The trick here is always to avoid the hype built around some of these companies. Instead, do adequate research on your own before buying into any of them.

- How to make tangible profits from your crypto-investment

I have vast knowledge about the Crypto & Blockchain space, and I am a passionate blockchain advocate. Fortunately, I have poured out years of experience within the cryptocurrency space into this book, which would surely help you navigate these problem areas.

Many crypto users see it as the future, and I believe that we have only begun to scratch the surface regarding the heights that these digital currencies can reach. Even though cryptocurrencies like Bitcoin have massively gained since it was first introduced more than a decade ago, the shared belief by many experts is that they would continue to appreciate in the coming years.

Meanwhile, other cryptocurrencies are also expected to appreciate over the next few years, so it is never too late to join the party. Thankfully, getting started in the crypto market is relatively easy, especially compared to the stock market. All you need to do is create a profile on one of the various platforms, get a digital wallet and begin to follow all your digital assets seamlessly.

The great news is that you have this book to guide you on this financial adventure. As you read through this book, make sure you keep David Foster Wallace's words to the graduating class at Kenyon College in 2005 -

"There are these two young fish swimming along, and they happen to meet an older fish swimming the other way, who nods at them and says, 'Morning, boys. How's the water?' And the two young fish swim on for a bit, and then eventually, one of them looks over and the other and says, "What's water?"

While explaining his water parable, Wallace revealed that the most obvious things about our lives and realities are often hidden in plain sight or within our grasp. Most times, it is just our perception about life that paints a picture of what is real or not real to every one of us.

Many people are limited from greatness by a lack of education, and unfortunately, the world is painfully wicked to those that choose to remain ignorant. Many people who have made huge losses from their cryptocurrency investment have been guilty of not doing their best to get adequate information about everything related to the cryptocurrency business.

As I mentioned earlier, there is very little information about cryptocurrency because most people are just there for the gains. And so, it is not so farfetched to come across someone who has been trading cryptocurrencies for many years but cannot give a formal lecture to potential crypto investors.

If there is anything I would like you to take with you as you flip through this book's pages, you must harness your hunger to learn and expand your horizon. As a writer and investor, I have found out that some issues tend to change as I learn about a topic. For example, there are many times I have wanted to respond during an argument hastily, but for some reason, I hold back. Then a few minutes later, I realize that I have a very different opinion from what I wanted to comment.

As you start this journey, my advice to you is to hold back on every thought or view you previously had about what cryptocurrency entails. I am not saying you should dismiss what you already know, but I urge you to keep them aside and open your mind to everything that I would explain in this book. As highlighted in Wallace's parable, everything about life is connected to how much understanding we have about our environment and things around us.

The cryptocurrency world is not any different, and your ability to thrive in this space is hinged on how well you can get yourself acquainted with all the variables. For example, the value of cryptocurrency is mainly determined by how much a buyer is willing to pay at a particular time. Therefore, you must arm yourself with basic knowledge of human behavior if you genuinely want to succeed as a crypto investor.

Some people have been in the crypto space for many years but continue to suffer heavy losses due to avoidable mistakes. While the cryptocurrency market might be an easy way to make new income on the side, it does not in any way diminish the level of complexity behind the blockchain technology that powers virtual currencies or its market dynamism.

When you pay due attention to cryptocurrency, it has a unique way of rewarding your effort. Consequently, you will be doing yourself a whole lot of good if you treat it with the seriousness that it deserves. So, allow me to take you on this journey!

What Is Cryptocurrency?

As we delve deeper into the world of virtual currencies, you must hold on to these earlier raised crucial points as they would help you on this financial adventure:

1. Cryptocurrency is a virtual medium of exchange that employs cryptographic functions to complete financial transactions. Digital currencies also use blockchain technology, which enables their transparency, immutability, and decentralization properties.

2. The most appealing feature of cryptocurrency for most users is that it is not controlled by any central figure, i.e., banks, organizations, or government institutions. In addition, the decentralized feature of the blockchain ensures that cryptocurrencies are theoretically immune to government interference or control.

3. Cryptocurrency is the first peer-to-peer currency and can be sent between people using private and public keys. Unlike traditional financial institutions that charge steep fees for transfers, cryptocurrency transactions can be completed with minimal processing fees. This feature has massively contributed to the growing popularity of crypto, as more people continue to swap traditional bank accounts for a crypto wallet.

Today, cryptocurrency is on the lips of almost everybody and continues to generate massive ripples within the global economic climate. The emergence of digital currencies over the last decade is arguably one of the more spectacular events that have taken place globally within that time frame. However, while cryptocurrency supporters continue to enjoy its many benefits and explore the endless possibilities linked to its use, the same cannot be said of most government authorities and banking institutions.

While some countries have kicked against the use of digital currencies, others have embraced it and even put policies in place that encourage their citizens to invest in crypto. Nevertheless, nothing reflects the significant influence of cryptocurrency over the global financial space other than the open obsession of banks, companies, and governments with it. As things stand, it is almost impossible not to find research based on cryptocurrency sponsored by one or more of these powerhouses.

During a 2013 Senate hearing to discuss the growing use of digital currencies, especially bitcoin, and whether the government was doing enough to "police" the market, Senator Thomas Carper, who chaired the committee, aptly describes the raucous surrounding cryptocurrency in his opening remarks. He said:

"Virtual currencies, perhaps most notably Bitcoin, have captured the imagination of some, struck fear among others, and confused the heck out of the rest of us."

The questions I am guessing are in everybody's mind at this point are:

- Why is there so much noise around cryptocurrency?
- Why is there still very little understanding of the basic concepts of cryptocurrency despite the noise and loud media coverage surrounding it?

In this chapter, I hope to shed more light on these questions and open your eyes to all you need to know about digital currencies and their intrinsic value to the global economic system. However, to fully understand the journey of cryptocurrency and its overwhelming popularity in recent years, you must first be aware of why it was created in the first place.

History of Cryptocurrency

As stated earlier, cryptocurrency is decentralized digital money, which is powered by blockchain technology. According to CoinLore, there are over 5,000 different digital currencies in circulation. However, the most popular versions are Bitcoin and Ethereum — the former being the first cryptocurrency created.

In a 2008 paper titled "Bitcoin: A Peer-to-Peer Electronic Cash System," Bitcoin creator Satoshi Nakamoto described the groundbreaking invention as "an electronic payment system based on cryptographic proof instead of trust." The following year Nakamoto introduced the first cryptocurrency, Bitcoin. Since then, more digital currencies have been created as the world rapidly gravitates towards a free-flowing cashless economy.

However, the mysterious Satoshi Nakamoto was not the first person to come up with the idea to create a cryptocurrency. American cryptographer David Chaum made the earliest dated contributions to this space with eCash and DigiCash in 1983 and 1995, respectively. At the time, the inventions leveraged cryptography to make economic transactions more confidential.

In 1998, the term "cryptocurrency" was coined and accomplished software engineer Wei Dai developed the framework for a new currency whose main characteristic would be decentralization. However, Wei Dai's invention "b-money" was never used as a form of exchange.

The late 1900s to the early 2000s were characterized by the sporadic rise of other conventional digital finance intermediaries. Among them was PayPal, which coincidentally made Tesla founder and cryptocurrency advocate Elon Musk's first fortune. The massive success of PayPal influenced most of the mobile payment technologies that have exploded into our lives today.

Despite the attempts of several people to crack open the digital currency space, the world would have to wait until 2009 before finally getting its first cryptocurrency.

Following the 2008 global economic crisis that affected everyone, including the powerhouses, people ultimately felt the need to take more control of their money.

Consequently, Bitcoin was introduced as a new, decentralized form of exchange that could be used internationally and without any financial institution behind it.

Despite the initial skepticism that greeted the introduction of cryptocurrency, Bitcoin had outperformed even the most favorable projections when it was created. In addition, the increasing acceptance of Bitcoin by the public led to the creation of other cryptocurrencies, which are collectively referred to as "altcoins."

What is "Big-Name" Crypto?

In early 2009, Satoshi Nakamoto introduced Bitcoin to the public and thus began a movement that has swept through the world and continues to generate contentious arguments, especially in the media, corporate and political corridors.

Despite the public anger and backlash towards the government and financial institutions, which emanated from the 2008 global financial crisis, there was still a lot of skepticism about Bitcoin. However, a group of dedicated supporters immediately jumped on the "new money" and began exchanging and mining the currency.

By late 2010, other similar cryptocurrencies — including popular alternatives like Litecoin — began to appear. Before 2010 all Bitcoin exchanges were done peer-to-peer, but the introduction of options like Litecoin barely preceded the first public Bitcoin exchange launch.

Barely two years later, the crypto space landed a significant boost when WordPress became the first prominent merchant to accept

Bitcoin payment. Over the last few years, others, including Microsoft, online electronics retailer Newegg.com, Expedia, and Tesla, have followed. While Bitcoin has not been certified a legal tender, many merchants and vendors now view the world's most popular cryptocurrency as a legitimate payment outlet.

Bitcoin continues to be the pacesetter for other cryptocurrencies. However, with more people entering the crypto space, a few cryptocurrencies apart from Bitcoin have been accepted for merchant payments and leave impressionable marks on global economics.

Today, Bitcoin, along with other cryptos, is being used to purchase common goods and services. Although crypto has become a convenient alternative to traditional currencies, it is still some way off from achieving true parity with the world's top fiat currencies. On the other hand, many people have made serious gains from investing in cryptocurrencies as they would in other assets, like stocks, gold, or forex.

Examples of "Big-Name" Cryptocurrencies

Since Bitcoin's release in 2009, cryptocurrency usage has exploded, and that trend looks set to continue into the foreseeable future. While there is a lot of uncertainty surrounding the exact number of currencies currently in circulation and individual currencies' values remain very volatile, all existing cryptocurrencies' overall market value is generally on the rise. As you read this, hundreds of cryptocurrencies are being traded actively.

Given the countless number of active cryptocurrencies, it would be impossible to discuss every one of them. The versions here are regarded as the "big-name" cryptocurrencies. They are robust user activity, stable adoption, and relatively high market capitalization (exceeding $10 million, in most instances, although valuations are subject to change per time):

Bitcoin

More than a decade after being introduced into the mainstream, Bitcoin remains the world's most widely used digital currency and is also credited with starting the crypto movement.

Its unit value and market capital constantly dwarves (by at least a factor of 10) that of the second most popular cryptocurrency. Most cryptocurrencies have a programmed supply limit, and that of Bitcoin is 21 million Bitcoin. More will be discussed on the finite supply of cryptocurrencies and why it was deemed necessary by the creators. Even though there is no official government support behind Bitcoin in most countries, it is increasingly regarded as a legitimate exchange form. As mentioned earlier, many big companies accept Bitcoin payments, albeit they partner with an exchange to convert Bitcoin to U.S. dollars before receiving the funds.

Ethereum

Ethereum (ETH) was launched in 2015 and has since become the second most popular cryptocurrency. In addition, it has consistently proven to be the second most valuable crypto behind only Bitcoin.

Since its creators had about six years to study Bitcoin's template, Ethereum made some significant improvements to Bitcoin's basic framework. Chief among these adjustments is that ETH uses "smart contracts" that guarantee the performance of a particular transaction, hold parties to their agreements and are equipped with mechanisms for refunds in the instance of one party violating the agreement.

While "smart contracts" go a long way in addressing the problems raised by a lack of chargebacks and refunds in the crypto space, there are still doubts about its overall capacity to provide a lasting solution. However, they are primarily responsible for Ethereum's success over the years.

Litecoin

It was released in 2011 and made use of the same basic architecture as Bitcoin, albeit with some slight disparities. Some of the significant differences that can be found in Litecoin (LTC) include an upgraded programmed supply limit (84 million units) and a faster target blockchain creation time (2.5 minutes).

Also, the encryption algorithm is marginally different from that of Bitcoin. Litecoin usually fluctuates between the second or third most popular cryptocurrency as per market capitalization.

Ripple

Released in 2012, Ripple (XRP) has enjoyed success despite steep competition from other cryptocurrencies. Noted for possessing a "consensus ledger" system that remarkably speeds up the rate transactions are completed and blockchain creation time — there is no specific time. Still, the recorded average hovers around a few seconds.

More importantly, Ripple enjoys better liquidity than other cryptocurrencies, thanks to an in-house currency exchange that readily converts Ripple units into currencies like U.S. dollars, yen, Euros, and other standard fiat currencies.

The main drawback of Ripple, as suggested by critics, is that its network and code are more vulnerable to attacks from sophisticated hackers and do not offer the same level of anonymity protection as Bitcoin-derived cryptocurrencies.

Dogecoin

Dogecoin (DOGE) is a slight variation of Litecoin, and its vastly famous Shiba Inu mascot denotes it. Dogecoin possesses some pretty severe upgrades to other cryptocurrencies that have allowed it to enjoy some level of success in the market away from the mascot business. Some of these features include a rapid blockchain creation time (one minute) and a more significant amount of coins in the market — as of July 2015, 100 billion units had been mined. After that, 5.2 billion units are mined every year without any known supply limit.

Dogecoin is seen as an experiment in "inflationary cryptocurrency," with experts keeping a close watch to see how it performs value-wise with other cryptocurrencies.

Several other cryptocurrencies are currently in the market, but those mentioned above five have been selected based on their "big-name" status and appeal to many users. The most significant power pull for these sets of cryptocurrencies can be seen in how major merchants are beginning to accept them as payment for their businesses.

The launch of Bitcoin in 2009 ushered in serious doubts about its acceptability and longevity. But if what has gone down in the last decade and what we see happening every day is anything to go by, then without mincing words, cryptocurrency is here to stay.

Since 2009, the market value of Bitcoin has skyrocketed, and a lot of early investors have made quite a fortune. Unsurprisingly such success has inadvertently rubbed off on other active cryptocurrencies, and their values are on a steady rise. From an expert point of view, cryptocurrency is a moving train with no stops in sight, so you will have to make that jump if you want to get into it.

I am here to provide a safe landing for you when you eventually decide to make that leap. This book will give you the edge you need to make informed decisions about how you want to go about your crypto journey. My advice for you is to do additional research about some other less popular cryptocurrencies that you can invest your money in because they are the most likely to give you the greatest return on your money within the shortest period.

But if you are looking to play it safe, you can try any of the cryptocurrencies above. Still, you must understand that these "big-name" cryptos periodically experience a "dip" in value, but time has shown that they always bounce back significantly. The world is being edged towards a free-flowing cashless economy by the enthusiastic younger generation. And with online purchases becoming a global trend, cryptocurrency cannot be better placed to claim more parity with the traditional payment systems.

However, while cryptocurrency retains its profile as an exciting new addition to the asset class, purchasing it poses a fair amount of risk as you must adequately research to grasp how each system works fully.

How Cryptocurrency Works

For most people, words like cryptocurrency, blockchain, and other crypto-linked terminologies are very likely to throw them off balance while trying to understand the system. And this comes as no surprise, given most people are more familiar with layman terms like money, checkbook, cash, etc., when it comes to their finances.

Additionally, the technical controls and source codes that enable and secure cryptocurrencies are pretty complex. However, it is within our limit to understand the basic concepts and become masterful users of cryptocurrency.

Several essential concepts govern cryptocurrencies' security, values, and integrity. To benefit those who are new to crypto, I will quickly highlight some of these concepts.

Cryptography

Digital currencies like Bitcoin use cryptographic protocols or very intricate code systems that encode sensitive data transfers to protect their exchange units. Crypto designers employ advanced mathematics and computer engineering principles to build these protocols — making them nearly impossible to break, copy or counterfeit the protected currencies.

These protocols also conceal the identities of crypto users on the various platforms they are registered with, thereby making transactions or funds flow impossible to pin on a specific group of persons.

Blockchain Technology

A blockchain can be described as an open, distributed ledger that stores transactions in codes. In practice, blockchain technology is more like our bank checkbooks that record a history of our dealings. The difference here is that records are scattered across an infinite number of computers across the globe. These transactions are stored in "blocks," tied through a "chain" of previous cryptocurrency transactions.

Thanks to the blockchain, every crypto user has a copy of their transaction history, which comes in a unified record. The software helps to log every new transaction as it happens. Every copy of the blockchain is updated with the latest information, ensuring that all documents are identical and accurate.

Typically, all cryptocurrency transactions are technically not completed until added to the blockchain, which usually takes a few minutes. Once the transaction is deemed successful, it is usually irreversible.

While other traditional payment platforms such as PayPal and credit cards, most digital currencies' designs have no built-in refund or chargeback functions. However, some newer versions of crypto have been built with rudimentary refund features.

During the few minutes between the transactions' initialization and completion, the units are held in a sort of limbo. They are unavailable for use by either the sender or the receiver. This essential feature helps prevent double-spending and protects the cryptocurrency units from being manipulated or duplicated to multiple recipients.

Decentralized Control

The essential characteristic of cryptocurrency is decentralized control which gives absolute power to the users.

Both the value and supply of cryptocurrencies are hinged on the activities of users and highly complex protocols designed into their governing codes rather than the efforts of central banks or other regulatory authorities.

The activities of miners — cryptocurrency users who skillfully use vast amounts of computing power to record transactions; receive newly created cryptocurrency units and transaction fees charged on other users — are crucial to the stability and smooth functioning of the various cryptocurrencies.

Private Keys

Before you can effectively call yourself a cryptocurrency user, you must have a private key. This private key authenticates your identity and enables you to exchange units on the crypto exchange platform of your choice.

Typically, users create their private keys, which are formatted as whole numbers up to 78 digits long. On the other hand, a random number generator can also be used to create a private key.

Once you have a key, you can acquire and spend cryptocurrency without any restrictions. You must understand that without this key, you will be unable to spend or convert your crypto. Your accumulated cryptocurrency is utterly useless without your key to activate and set them in motion.

While this is a crucial security feature limiting theft and unauthorized use, it is also a tad draconian. Losing this key can be accurately compared to throwing a wad of cash into a fiery furnace and watching it disappear into dark smoke.

Of course, you can create another private key and begin building your cryptocurrency wallet again. But you can never recover the crypto asset protected by the old lost key. This is why experienced cryptocurrency users are obsessively protective of their private keys and are known to store them in multiple non

internet connected digital locations, including paper and other physical forms.

Cryptocurrency Wallets

Cryptocurrency wallets can be likened to the bank account that houses your money. While private keys are used to authenticate a cryptocurrency transaction, wallets primarily serve to secure the crypto units that are not in use from potential theft.

However, the wallets used by the numerous crypto exchanges are still quite vulnerable to hacking. For example, Japan-based Bitcoin exchange Mt. Gox had to shut down and declare bankruptcy some years back after hackers systematically stole over $450 million in Bitcoin exchanged from its servers.

Unlike traditional financial institutions that require physical addresses to operate, crypto wallets can be stored in an internal hard drive, external hard drive, or on the cloud. But, regardless of where you choose to store your wallet, the ideal thing is to make sure you have at least one backup for it.

However, you must understand that creating a backup for your wallet does not duplicate the existing cryptocurrency units but just the record of their existence and current ownership.

Miners

Miners are another significant group of people in the virtual currency ecosystem. They can be described as the record-keepers in this system, and their actions indirectly influence the currencies' value.

As stated earlier, miners use vast computing resources often domiciled in large private server farms owned by mining groups that consist of several individuals. To achieve their objectives, they use highly complex methods to authenticate the accuracy, completeness, and security of currencies' blockchains.

Apart from periodically creating new copies of the blockchain by completing previously unverified transactions, the term "miners" relates to their capacity to generate wealth by injecting brand-new cryptocurrency units into the system.

There is more to the activities of miners as they form an essential core in the cryptocurrency world. However, their operations require a sizable investment, and that is not the scope of this book. So, for now, let's focus on getting you acquainted with the cryptocurrency world so you can hopefully start making some helpful side money on your own in no time.

Finite Supply

Although the activities of miners periodically produce new cryptocurrency units, most digital currencies are pre-designed to have a finite supply — a significant guarantor of value.

In practice, what this means is that miners would be unable to create new units at some point. The good news is that based on current trends and projections, the last Bitcoin unit would be mined around the mid-22nd century — not exactly going to happen anytime soon, so there is still enough time to grab a few coins.

The finite supply of cryptocurrencies places them more in the class of gold and other precious metals — which also have limited supply — than fiat currencies that are controlled by central banks, who, in theory, can produce these currencies at will.

Cryptocurrency Exchanges

At this point, you have some information about cryptocurrency, and you are anxious to get into the market to test your understanding about this space, or at least before we run out of supply of Bitcoin.

Hold on; we are still in the 21st century. Besides, cryptocurrency exchanges may not be as complex as crypto itself. Still, your understanding of how it works will go a long way in determining how profitable this journey will be for you.

At the bottom of the crypto space, many lesser-used cryptocurrencies can only be exchanged via private, peer-to-peer transfers. Consequently, they are pretty challenging to liquidate, and determining their value concerning other currencies — both crypto and fiat — is always a tough ask.

For more popular cryptocurrencies such as Bitcoin, Ethereum, and Ripple, are traded on notable secondary exchanges similar to forex exchanges for fiat currencies. The now-defunct Mt. Gox is an excellent example of an exchange.

These exchanges allow users to trade their cryptocurrency units for major fiat currencies like the U.S. dollar and Euro. There is also the option to exchange their crypto holdings for other lesser cryptocurrencies. These companies take a small cut from every transaction for their services, usually less than 1% of each transaction's value.

Also, cryptocurrency can be traded for fiat currencies in unique online markets. Each cryptocurrency has a determined variable exchange rate with significant fiat currencies, including the U.S. dollar, European Euro, British Pound, and Japanese Yen.

Cryptocurrency exchanges play a crucial role in liquid ability and determine their value concerning major world fiat currencies. However, this system is still highly volatile.

A case in point is how Bitcoin's U.S. dollar exchange rate "dipped" more than 50% following the collapse of Mt. Gox in 2014, then increased nearly tenfold in 2017 as the demand for cryptocurrency exploded.

Finally, keep in mind that cryptocurrency exchanges are still quite vulnerable to hackers. The case of Mt. Gox remains a painful reminder of the threat of cybercriminals and the need for heightened cybersecurity and awareness.

Can Anyone Buy Cryptocurrency?

Yes! Any adult can buy cryptocurrency. However, that largely depends on such individuals' mental health and, more importantly, living in a country that allows its citizens to do business with crypto.

Despite the apprehension from the United States government about the risks involved in cryptocurrency, there is no doubt that their use is legal in America. However, there have been conversations in the U.S. Congress about the lack of adequate policing of the crypto space.

Countries like China have gone a step further to ban cryptocurrencies, as they believe the continued use by their citizens could have adverse effects on their economy. Ultimately, the legality of crypto and your ability to spend or buy cryptocurrency depend on each country's government.

Aside from government restrictions in individual countries, anyone anywhere in the world is free to buy cryptocurrency. However, before you buy any digital currency, make sure you consider ways to protect yourself from fraudsters looking to exploit naive investors.

Several cryptocurrencies, including Bitcoin, are available for purchase with popular fiat currencies like U.S. dollars, while others require that you purchase them with Bitcoins or any other top cryptocurrency. It is pretty easy to buy cryptocurrency once you qualify as an adult. The first thing you need to do is open up a wallet — an online app that keeps your cryptocurrency holdings.

Typically, you are to create a profile on an exchange, and then you can make use of real money to purchase cryptocurrencies such as Bitcoin or Ethereum. I will discuss how you can buy a cryptocurrency and the different platforms at your disposal in the next chapter.

There are so many reasons you should invest in cryptocurrency, as discussed throughout this chapter. But primarily, their political independence and defiant data security allow crypto users to enjoy benefits that traditional fiat currencies, such as the U.S. dollar, rarely ever experience.

For example, while a government can readily block or even go ahead to seize a bank account domiciled in its jurisdiction, it is nearly impossible to take out the same action with funds held in cryptocurrency. Whether or not the holder of such funds is a citizen or legal resident of that country.

Finally, I would be doing you no favors if I don't emphasize that cryptocurrencies have some risks and drawbacks, such as illiquidity and value volatility, which don't affect most top fiat currencies. This is the more reason why you must do your research to know exactly how you want to come into the crypto space — whether as a short-term investor or you are in it for the long haul.

Additionally, due to the confidentiality of cryptocurrencies, they are frequently used by criminals to facilitate illicit and black market transactions. This is why so many countries have a heightened level of distrust or feel outright animosity towards the various cryptocurrencies in the market.

It is believed that if crypto creators could work on these gray areas while still maintaining users' anonymity, they would have gone a long way in scoring a significant point towards becoming a recognized legal tender. But before then, there is no doubt that cryptocurrency has become a valuable way of making some tangible side money. Many people have already taken advantage of the trend, and believe me, nothing is stopping you except a lack of information and fear!

How Do I Get Crypto?

Over the past few weeks, the media and airwaves have been dominated by talks surrounding the market performance of cryptocurrencies like Ethereum, Dogecoin, and Shiba Inu coin. The trio has experienced a rapid rise in its value, and the incredible feat even made it onto Saturday Night Live. While these upstarts seem to be hugging the headlines nowadays, we must not forget their predecessor — the relatively stable and borderline boring original cryptocurrency, Bitcoin.

Yes, I did not stutter: Bitcoin is a bit boring. Boring is never wrong, especially when you are dealing with crypto. In fact, on the side of the investor, boring is an excellent prerequisite to guaranteed success in any of their dealings. As a newbie investor in cryptocurrency, it is always advisable to go safe while learning the ropes, and in this regard, Bitcoin is the best bet.

It has been 12 years since Bitcoin was created, and it has established itself as the blue-chip stock of the emerging cryptocurrency asset class. The jury is still out on whether it is the safest investment in the crypto space, but without a doubt, it is the one most likely to be still going strong in the long term. It claims the most used digital currency worldwide by a wide margin — with roughly half a million active users initiating at least 300,000 transactions every day.

More importantly, it still holds the best store of value compared to other crypto assets, as it accounts for roughly $1 trillion. And given the current trends, there is nothing that suggests it would not continue to gain supporters and users, thereby appreciating as time goes on.

Despite earning a "boring" tag, Bitcoin still experiences dips in price, including a massive price fall in May 2021. However, given how a vast majority of people globally have become somewhat dependent on cryptocurrency, the store of value that Bitcoin embodies is not simply necessary but has become increasingly part of the skeletal frame of the global economy. It is believed that it is only a matter of time before Bitcoin finally joins the mainstream for most experts.

An old but common expression explains the importance of buying the fruit just before it gets ripe rather than waiting for it to get ripe before you make your move. Over the years, you must have heard many crypto experts on social media advising people to buy the "dip." In this case, it is just a passionate call out for intended investors to take advantage of a fall in the price of a popular cryptocurrency to purchase as many units as possible because it is almost certain to bounce back to its previous price with time.

Besides taking advantage of a dip to buy cryptocurrency, the other option available to you to make a sizable profit on your crypto investment is to get in early. Those who invested in the early days of Bitcoin and were able to hold off from selling their units would be smiling wildly to the bank at this moment, thanks to the unprecedented rise in the value of Bitcoin. Interestingly, the total value has already exceeded 10% of that of gold. I regularly get asked why I invest in Bitcoin, and every time my response is the same.

Imagine you had a young daughter, whom you love very much, and you have tasked yourself to save for her future. You know that one day, she will turn 18 and jet off to college. But how can you transfer some money into the future to ensure your daughter has all that she needs at 18? A prom dress? A car? A college education?

This is the primary objective behind most savings and investments — to ensure value is transferred into the future— and Bitcoin has proven to be quite adept at it because of its limited supply. As stated previously, there will only be a finite amount of Bitcoins created (21 million), so the chances of its value appreciating, or at the least holding steady, is overwhelming.

When I began my crypto journey in 2010, just a few people outside the founding circle and some other technology enthusiasts had ever heard of Bitcoin. Two years down the line, I turned away from a comfortable corporate path to pursue an unknown business in an unfamiliar industry. While many people felt I had probably lost my mind or something, deep down, I had this firm conviction that Bitcoin would change the world as we knew it.

So I stubbornly continued adding to my Bitcoin wallet because I was convinced the price — less than $10 when I began — was bound to take off at some point. More importantly, I made up my mind to turn a blind eye to its volatility.

Last year, during the pandemic-induced economic collapse that saw the price of Bitcoin fall in March of 2020, I saw a rare opportunity to acquire more at a price I was sure may never happen again — so I did!

I will take the same approach when there is another dip in price due to panic selling. However, when Bitcoin attains a level that I can achieve profitability of at least 100 times my initial investment, I will be more than willing to sell and claim my profit, rather than following the crowd who jumped in at first sight of an increase.

The most important lesson to pick from all of these for the intended Bitcoin investor is this — which is more or less like any other conventional investing advice: If you painstakingly research an investment, then go ahead and invest with patience mostly pay off.

Now that we have put all that stuff out in the open, the next step is to get to know how you can get your hands on some cryptocurrency units.

Let's face it – the major financial trend right now is that everyone is trying to earn some cryptocurrency one way or the other. Nobody wants to miss out on the significant profits realized from the spikes in the price of crypto coins. However, the cryptocurrency market is highly volatile. As much as the gains could be pretty tempting, most responsible adults with tough real

life decisions to make do not want to risk losing their hard-earned money.

I know how difficult it is when you are just getting into something that can be as confusing as investing in cryptocurrency. Apart from the availability of thousands of versions, several platforms offer different values for your money when buying crypto. This book was written to give you an edge and prevent you from making avoidable mistakes.

With that said, here are some of the best ways that I know you can acquire some crypto coins at a minimum risk (and sometimes effort).

Buying

This is by far the most straightforward way to earn cryptocurrency. Thankfully, buying crypto has gotten easier over the years, and right now, you can readily get crypto from the comfort of your home within a few minutes.

As the popularity of cryptocurrency increased through the years, so did its demand. Several companies collectively called "exchanges" began offering services that allowed people to enter the crypto market safely and without unnecessary hassles.

So how can you buy cryptocurrency?

For example, buying Bitcoin has gotten so easy you can go to a Bitcoin ATM and bring it with some cash or credit. Other coins may not be accessible, but you can get them through the crypto exchanges I mentioned earlier. But bear in mind that there are transaction fees attached to every purchase.

These transaction fees are consistently updated on most exchanges to reflect the current market value of individual crypto coins. However, these fees are pretty low and very affordable.

In contrast, the transaction fees charged for purchasing Bitcoin via the ATM are on the high side, so I always advise that you buy your Bitcoin or other cryptocurrencies using exchanges like Binance, Coinbase, or Kraken. In most cases, the process is relatively straightforward and takes only a few minutes from start to finish. All you have to do is sign-up for an account on any of the active exchanges, verify it, and you are good to go!

In some cases, some exchanges put up extra security measures by requesting verification from your bank before the process is finalized. Inadvertently, that will extend the process by a few more weeks at best.

So if you are in a hurry, it is advisable that you check the sign up and verification process of the exchange that you decide to use, or just buy your cryptocurrency units with cash directly from the ATM.

1. Start Mining Crypto

Mining is another excellent way to earn some cryptocurrency, but it is not possible for all currencies. Most people erroneously believe mining is all about snatching or grabbing as many crypto coins as possible for yourself. However, the whole process is more complicated than that, and as the name denotes, there is a lot of work involved in mining. A miner solves complex mathematical problems that help authenticate blocks of transactions. All cryptocurrencies already exist inside a protocol but need to be established before they can be available on the market. The first person that can complete the authentication process gets rewarded with a fragment of the virtual token he authenticated.

2. How Easy is Mining?

First off, you must be clear about what you intend to mine. For instance, Bitcoin mining requires very high-tech equipment like ASIC (Application-Specific Integrated Circuit), while other cryptocurrencies can be mined using regular computers.

However, if you are adamant about mining Bitcoin, you don't need to invest thousands of dollars before you can get started. My advice is to join a mining network, which only requires that you pay a joining fee. This will allow you to work with other more experienced members, who you can learn from in the long run. However, you will have to split the reward with other members of the group. Meanwhile, some of the best cryptos that you can mine at the moment are:

- Ethereum (ETH)
- Dash (DASH)
- Monero (XMR)
- Litecoin (LTC)

3. Get Crypto by Staking

If you are interested in getting some crypto coins and, for some reason, the two previous options do not work for you — have no fear. There is still a way to get them.

There are two main methods used to authenticate blocks — Proof of Work and Proof of Stake.

While PoW is dependent on users mining blocks and finalizing transactions through sheer computational power, PoS takes an entirely different route.

For the PoS method, the user to create a new block is picked in a deterministic way, mainly due to the number of coins the individual already holds.

As the name denotes, staking is a lot like a lottery game. The chances of you getting chosen to authenticate a transaction improve with the number of coins you have and willing to put into staking. Consequently, this method is excellent for those who are looking to increase their crypto holdings.

4. Get Crypto with Defi Yield Farming

Also referred to as Yield Farming or Liquidity Mining, a reward system bears an uncanny resemblance with what can be obtained in the bonds market.

In plain terms, Yield Farming is a method of obtaining rewards by locking up cryptocurrencies for a specific period and simultaneously granting liquidity to a Defi token. Some of the most recognized Defis that can be mined right now are:

- Compound (COMP)
- Kyber Network (KNC)
- Ox (ZRX)
- Ren (REN)

5. Join a Few Airdrops to get Crypto Coins

Airdrops are a great way of always putting yourself at the center of information, so you can always take advantage of emerging projects.

For those of us within this space, it is no secret that most projects use airdrops campaigns to create awareness about their product and attract traffic back to it. This is an excellent method because it enables crypto enthusiasts to be notified about upcoming projects while at the same time providing them with something valuable — tokens.

In exchange for performing specific tasks, users are rewarded with some of the project's tokens.

Once the project reaches its target market, those tokens can be exchanged for other coins or sold for cash. Here are a few of the most common tasks you will find:

- Following social media channels
- Sharing social media posts
- Registering on their platform
- Downloading their app

6. Use Microtasks to Promote Projects

They are commonly known as "Bounties" but are very similar to airdrops. Together with the latter, they may be the most straightforward way to earn crypto.

Today, many businesses and startups offer crypto as a reward to anyone to complete various tasks. However, microtasks are a bit more complex than airdrops when placed side by side. Here, the tasks are primarily promotional and can include any of the following:

- Writing a testimonial
- Creating a video review
- Writing a press release
- Distributing a promotional video

Several websites provide a listing of available Bounties and airdrops, so if you are looking to earn some emerging crypto coins, you can make your way to the following pages:

- 99 Airdrops
- Airdrops Alert
- Bounties Alert

7. Get Paid in Bitcoins for Freelance jobs

You have the option of taking microtasks a notch higher by choosing to get paid in Bitcoin or other cryptocurrencies for jobs done. Today, several platforms facilitate freelancing via blockchain technology. And the good thing is that most of these platforms do not charge any transaction fees, so workers receive precisely what the employer pays.

More people are joining the freelance community each day due to the many benefits attached to it. And if the risk of accepting payment in Bitcoin seems to be too much for you, then you can go for a more stable cryptocurrency. If this particular method interests you, then here are a few places to try out:

- Enhance
- Cryptocurrency jobs

8. Accept Cryptocurrency Payments

If you are an entrepreneur and own an e-commerce website, then this option is tailor-made for you. *Why?* Platforms such as WooCommerce and Shopify have made it possible for vendors to accept crypto coins as payment via their websites. And the great thing is, these platforms allow several types of crypto as payment.

For example, WooCommerce allows its clients to accept more than 50 cryptocurrencies as payment, while Shopify takes it up a notch by allowing over 300 altcoins. More importantly, the process is relatively straightforward!

For Shopify, all that is required is that you switch to an alternative payment method on your Shopify account. Meanwhile, for WooCommerce, you will need to install an additional plugin like BitPay or CoinGate. Once installed, activate and configure it, then you are good to go.

9. Find and Join a Network of Publishers

Even if your website is not for e-commerce, you can still earn some crypto coins from it. Given that Google passed a ban and local crypto-related businesses from sponsoring ads through its network, the advertising industry was pressed to adapt.

A host of crypto ad networks (like coinzilla) have stepped in to fill the market's advertising needs. These platforms created robust networks of crypto publishers, which allows advertisers to put up their banners.

In exchange for showing off the ads, the publisher gets paid. While most of the networks still pay their users using fiat currencies like U.S. dollars or Euro, many platforms make payments in cryptocurrency.

10. Make Use of Cryptocurrency and Payment Platforms

As I have said several times throughout this book, the world is increasingly tilting towards a cashless era dominated by digital banking — and cryptocurrency is at the center of it all.

Many cryptocurrency and payment platforms (like crypto.com) offer financial management programs to help you acquire more crypto coins by using the units already in your possession.

Apart from getting crypto coins from the usual banking actions like depositing and picking up the interest, you can also benefit from cashback functionalities.

Every individual has daily, weekly and monthly expenditures, and in some cases, they are recurring. Why not gain some of your money back while paying these bills using a card from these fintech companies.

For crypto.com, you can make up to 5% back from all your expenditures by using the Metal Visa Card. The crypto industry is vast and presents a host of opportunities without any discrimination. There are some other ways to earn crypto, but what I have done here is to select the safest methods to try carefully. But remember that you will need to open a crypto wallet before you can get your hands on those crypto coins. For that, the internet is at your disposal to do your research and choose a suitable crypto exchange platform that aligns with your goals.

Apart from these methods of earning cryptocurrency, some other ways of getting crypto that I like to describe as dark methods are frowned upon.

So what are these dark methods? Cryptocurrency is yet to break into the mainstream. Still, sadly it has already been trailed by an unwelcome narrative — that an individual or even an entire crypto exchange platform can be subject to malicious hacks. For every crypto user, the risks of theft and vulnerability to hackers who try to earn cryptocurrencies by breaking into computer networks that hold your assets is a reality that you must live with.

The 2014 viral story of how now-defunct high-profile exchange Mt. Gox declared bankruptcy after hackers made away with hundreds of millions of dollars in Bitcoins from the platform, further painting the severity of the threat posed by online thieves and hackers the overall growth of cryptocurrency.

What further complicates this theft is the anonymity that has made cryptocurrencies so desirable in the first place. So, a large quantity of cryptocurrency goes missing, and the hackers seem to disappear into thin air with no digital footprint to track them. Like the case of 2014, these digital assets can never be recovered or even traced.

The story of digital asset theft, especially when it comes to crypto, has become a common theme that threatens to slow down the rate of acceptance of cryptocurrency. Many investors are understandably skeptical about investing their money without any assurance that it is safe from hackers. After all, these are not the typical risks they come across when investing in stocks and funds on notable U.S. exchanges.

While the crypto space continues to grow exponentially, the methods by which online thieves and hackers perpetuate their dastardly acts have also become more sophisticated. However, careful and prepared investors can successfully put preventive measures in place to safeguard their digital assets.

How do I protect myself? Before buying cryptocurrency in an ICO, thoroughly peruse the fine details in the company's description for the following:

- Who are the founders of the company? An identifiable owner with an excellent social profile is a positive sign.
- How many other prominent investors have their money tied to it? It is a positive sign if other well-known investors are part of the company.
- Are there provisions for you to own a stake in the company, or are you just limited to currency and tokens? It is an important distinction that you must clarify. When you own a stake, you get to partake in its earnings (you are an owner), while buying tokens limits you only to their use.
- How developed is the currency, or is the company still sourcing funds to develop it? The longer the product has existed in the market, the less likely it is to fail or burst.

It can be quite tasking to painstakingly go through every fine detail of a company's prospectus. However, the more detailed it is, the more likely that it is legitimate. Still, legitimacy does not give any assurances that the currency will be a success in the market. That is a whole topic on its own and requires a deep understanding of how the market works.

How Many Crypto Can I Buy?

With so many stories of people making millions of dollars in profits from their investment in cryptocurrency dominating social media throughout the last months of 2020, the new year ushered in a crowd of crypto enthusiasts looking to partake in the crypto largesse.

With thousands of cryptocurrencies being traded publicly, and the most popular digital currency, Bitcoin, has a price value that was on the high side; newbie crypto users. Those looking to cash in quickly were faced with the tough decision of which of the other cryptocurrencies to invest in for maximum profit.

Most of them found it challenging to choose because they did not have enough knowledge about the crypto space to make an informed decision. And so, they took the following line of action typical of someone confused — invest in multiple cryptocurrencies.

Yes, no law says you cannot invest in multiple cryptocurrencies, but without a deep understanding of precisely what you are doing, there's a very high tendency for you to lose a lot of money. And since you have invested in multiple currencies, I do not need to spell out that your losses would also come in many folds. So when I get asked by newbie crypto users if it is best to invest in multiple cryptocurrencies or just one, my answer is always the same — first get the knowledge you need about the crypto space, then start with baby steps before you make the jump.

Most of us have spent the better part of our lives learning about money and how to manage our finances, but when it comes to cryptocurrency, we just want to rush into it without any knowledge of the market. Some go ahead to invest their hard-earned money based on a false sense of what they perceive the crypto space is like.

There is no shortcut to investing in cryptocurrency. Neither is there a "one size fits all" approach to the crypto space. The sober truth is that you need to put in the work to learn the basics before you make your move.

Also to know just where you are, here are a few questions you need to ask yourself before you invest in any cryptocurrencies in 2021:

- Can you afford to lose your money if the cryptocurrency you invest in crashes?
- Are you merely curious about cryptocurrencies and the crypto space, or are you ready to invest?
- Do you have an actionable plan as well as a strategy for how you intend to build your crypto portfolio?
- Are you only interested in making a quick profit by buying & selling or keeping your assets long-term or a combination of both?

My candid advice is if you do not have precise answers to every question asked above, and you proceed to invest in cryptocurrency, then you have just gone into this marketplace blind. With "luck," you could make money, but you are more likely to lose your investment.

Finally, I would like you to try a quick experiment. I need you to head over to the busiest part of your home, then get a blindfold and tie it over your eyes, making sure everything is pitch black. The next task is to navigate around that space and out the door to another room without bumping into anything.

Now you see the difficulty level of that exercise. Even though you are very familiar with that room, it is still nearly impossible to successfully navigate the room with your eyes blindfolded. Many people have been doing this in the crypto market that quickly leads them to make substantial financial losses.

You must respect the digital currency market and research all the facts you need. But in any case, you have already taken the first step in the right direction by reading this book.

How Many Cryptocurrencies Are There?

Since the turn of the century, technology has given new life and meaning to everything we do. Consequently, the ways by which we go about our daily affairs have changed dramatically – learning, doing business, staying connected with family and friends, and of course – trading. A key breakthrough in technology first provided us with the ease of online payments. Additionally, trading online has been made possible via credit or debit cards, or payment services, such as Paypal, or using digital currencies.

As of 2019, the global cryptocurrency market size was pegged at an impressive USD 754.0 million. Despite the incredible numbers in such a short lifespan, experts are still quite optimistic about the prospects of virtual currencies, and they have projected the crypto market size to reach USD 1,758.0 million by 2027 — thereby showing a CAGR of 11.2% during the estimated period.

Technology continues to be the vehicle that drives cryptocurrencies' push for mainstream acceptance. The proliferation of virtual currency exchange methods has made it easier for people to buy and sell various cryptocurrencies quickly.

The introduction of exchanges into the crypto space has exposed crypto users to more business opportunities rather than demonstrable transactions in social and gaming economies. These improvements have not gone unnoticed, with most developing countries like the United States of America, Germany, and the U.K. already starting to adopt digital currencies as an exchanging medium.

At the forefront of the cryptocurrency revolution is the biggest of all digital currencies, Bitcoin. Over the last few years, Bitcoin has earned a reputation for its volatility and strongly bounced back in 2020, following its famous crash in 2018. From mid-March last year to February 2021, crypto users witnessed Bitcoin's value surge dramatically by roughly 800 percent.

The value of Bitcoin reached all-time highs during mid February and even surpassed the $57,000 mark. Even though the price has since plunged — as has happened many times in the past — experts believe that the digital currency will still experience a more significant surge in price later this year.

More importantly, several favorable investors are putting high stakes on Bitcoin's chances of becoming a mainstream asset. Unsurprisingly, these positive reviews have inspired many potential investors looking to get their hands on some Bitcoin units.

The recent price surges experienced have undoubtedly re awakened consumer interest in cryptocurrency, which seemed to have waned since Bitcoin's famous fall in 2018.

Consequently, other cryptocurrencies such as Ethereum and the enigmatic Dogecoin, have been enjoying an unprecedented level of patronage from crypto enthusiasts and potential investors.

Since its creation in 2009, Bitcoin is dubbed the "currency of the future" by supporters, which hasn't stopped skeptics from pointing to its flaws. Bitcoin has become a very polarizing topic, with public opinion still fiercely divided. However, such scenarios only increase the popularity of Bitcoin with each passing day.

The increased acceptance of digital currencies like Bitcoin, Ethereum, and Litecoin is likely to inspire rapid market growth in the next few years. Crucially, crypto coins are powered by blockchain technology, responsible for decentralization, and guarantees controlled, efficient transactions.

Apart from a decentralized system, other benefits of blockchain technology include fast, secure, reliable, and transparent transactions. With these advantages, it is no surprise that companies are adopting cryptocurrency as a means of payment for their services. This has ultimately contributed to the increasing popularity of digital currencies, and there seems to be no slowing down at the moment.

Other important reasons why the cryptocurrency is gaining popularity amongst potential investors include:

1. The Pandemic Effect

The popularity of Bitcoin suffered a massive blow in 2018 and struggled to get back on track throughout 2019. However, it started picking up speed during 2020 — described by the IMF as the year of the "Great Lockdown."

At the beginning of 2020, the world was hit by the novel coronavirus pandemic that tore through economies across the globe. After authorities struggled to curb the spread of the highly contagious virus with little success, they had no choice but to impose strict lockdowns and travel bans.

Understandably, this action took a devastating toll on the world economy, and all types of mainstream investments and assets also took a big hit. Once again, the world was faced with another financial disaster in the form of the global financial crisis of 2008. Suddenly, international investors were confronted by the same fear that led to the creation of Bitcoin in 2009 — only this time it had set the stage for a revival!

Financial disaster is a phenomenon that periodically plagues traditional banking and the financial sector. When there is an air of uncertainty around the finances of individuals, it has a ripple effect on the economy by causing the currency to fall. However, Bitcoin and other cryptocurrencies are generally immune to the impact of any financial crisis as their values are balanced across borders.

This particular quality makes cryptocurrencies the best bet for investors, especially those in geographic regions characterized by financial uncertainty and unstable economic structure. Over the years, these factors have proven to be a significant catalyst for the growth of the crypto space, last year, there was a repeat of such a scenario as the COVID-19 pandemic aggressively tore through world economies.

The cryptocurrency that had only been written off by some experts a few years ago took a complete u-turn and began to surge as many investors as possible. Companies rushed to stockpile cryptocurrency during the pandemic.

According to cryptocurrency experts, more global investment securities are now turning to digital currencies as an alternative asset to the conventional ones like gold, money, and equities. During a recent interview with Bloomberg, managing partner and co-founder of Nexo in London, Antoni Trenchev explained that Bitcoin has expanded beyond the circle of "tech geeks" and market speculators.

Additionally, Global investment bank and financial services provider JP Morgan Chase and Co have backed Bitcoin to experience a sharp rise in value in the long-term, provided that volatility can be kept under control.

2. Investors Made More from Bitcoin During the Pandemic

As the novel coronavirus pandemic forced a global lockdown, economic activities were brought to a halt, and many investors turned to safe havens like gold to secure their money as the financial sector fought for dear life. On the other hand, some investors opted to put their money in the less traditional Bitcoin.

Well, both sets of investors gained. However, those who invested in Bitcoin made the most profits — in fact, four times more than what gold investors gained.

Inspired by the testimonies of their counterparts, today, more investors are considering investing in Bitcoin or other cryptocurrencies rather than gold. Still, such a development would most likely occur over an extended period, given the enormous market capitalization of gold.

3. Finite Supply

The limited supply of Bitcoin (and most cryptocurrencies) available to the public is another reason behind the craze in demand being witnessed recently. As stated earlier, the collection of Bitcoin is limited to 21 million — already 18 million coins have been mined and are currently in circulation.

Bitcoin's finite supply made it immune to the effects of the pandemic, unlike the traditional fiat currencies that experienced dramatic falls due to more money been printed.

4. Quick and Cheaper transactions

When making transfers with cryptocurrencies, transaction fees charged are significantly cheaper compared to other traditional fiat currencies.

In international money transfers, which usually take from a few days to more than a week to be completed, cryptocurrency transactions are finalized within an hour.

This is since Bitcoin and other digital currencies are completely global and are decentralized, making them subject to very few laws and restrictions that are standard practices for banking institutions.

5. Widespread Usage

Another critical factor behind the increased popularity of digital currencies is their widespread usage across the world. The existence of several crypto exchanges has improved the liquid ability of digital currencies and made it possible to do more with your coins, including making payments for services.

Cryptocurrency also offers increased ease to its consumers while performing transactions, in addition to heightened security when compared to credit or debit cards that are known to be prone to such risks as fraud and identity theft during online trading.

More importantly, the popularity of digital currencies among consumers has skyrocketed due to the increasing number of businesses that have accepted Bitcoin as a means of payment. Crypto acceptance can also be felt in our real-life daily routines. Local businesses like coffee shops, restaurants, real estate companies and many other small-scale companies now accept Bitcoin for payment.

With the value and popularity of Bitcoin on the rise, it is a no-brainer that the number of businesses and merchants that accept Bitcoin would also continue to increase.

It has genuinely been an incredible journey of a decade for Bitcoin, but the last twelve months have been crucially important to the success of cryptocurrency as a mainstream asset. And 2021 is shaping up to hold more value in-store, not just for Bitcoin but the whole digital currency family.

The 2021 Cryptocurrency Revolution

The crypto revolution has been in the works for some time now, but to say that 2021 has so far been a significant year for Bitcoin and other cryptocurrency adoption would be a gross misstatement of facts. Over the last few months, the crypto space has experienced tremendous growth, with several big-name companies deciding to join the crypto train.

The world is currently witnessing a significant shift away from conventional financial institutions. We see big-money companies like Tesla coming out to endorse Bitcoin and alert their consumers they can now do business with their company using Bitcoin. Back in February, Tesla stunned the finance world when it announced it bought $1.5 billion worth of bitcoin. The move was made to ensure more flexibility and diversify and maximize the returns on their cash. It was a big statement by Tesla led by their billionaire inventor Elon Musk, and it earned him plaudits within the industry. Meanwhile, the value of Bitcoin experienced a massive surge soon after.

That same month, MasterCard also announced its plans to offer vendors the option to receive payments in cryptocurrency later this year. To emphasize how massive the year has been for the crypto space, several other notable financial services companies like PayPal, Venmo, and Square, also rolled out their plans to adopt cryptocurrency as means of payment.

Before the pandemic, cryptocurrency was experiencing a bit of a dull patch, with critics getting ever so confident about their doubts on digital currencies making it to the mainstream. However, the gains made by investors during the pandemic caused a storm on social media throughout 2020.

The cryptocurrency space carried all of that momentum into 2021. Investors began to shift their attention from traditional investment options to purchase different versions of the digital currencies in the market. With the spotlight on the crypto space again, it was not much of a big surprise to see leading companies begin to accept cryptocurrencies as a payment option. It makes a lot of sense when one looks at it from a business angle.

However, what has surprised most people is the vocal support that some big companies, especially Tesla, have shown for cryptocurrency. Elon Musk and his company have been among the most significant influences during Bitcoin's most recent resurgence. Every time the Tesla Chief executive has spoken or tweeted about Bitcoin, there has always been a tsunami of reactions both in the social media and financial spaces.

Earlier in January, Musk sent the prices of Bitcoin soaring by nearly 20% when he added "#bitcoin" to his Twitter biography. The following month, Musk caused the value of Bitcoin to rise by 16% in just one day after Tesla Inc. announced that it purchased $1.5 billion worth of Bitcoin.

Following that move, the value of Bitcoin saw a dramatic increase and peaked at almost during mid-April. At this point, the popularity of Bitcoin was soaring high, and buoyed by the acceptance it was getting from other leading companies, it seemed like Bitcoin was finally getting a much-deserved shot at the mainstream.

However, Musk showed how much of an influence he had on Bitcoin when he took to his official Twitter account earlier in May to reveal that Tesla would no longer accept Bitcoin as a means of payment for their vehicles. That single tweet sparked a massive selloff that has erased Bitcoin's gains since January and wiped out hundreds of billions of dollars from its market capitalization.

Within a week of Musk's tweet, the value of Bitcoin fell by nearly 40%. However, that has not impacted Bitcoin's popularity in any way, with most crypto supporters still very confident that the digital currency would rise again this year and even exceed the $65,000 mark.

Consequently, several campaigns by crypto users and supporters urge people to buy the "dip" in anticipation of future gains. So, despite Bitcoin's slump, it is still enjoying massive popularity worldwide as many people scramble to buy as many units as they can afford while the price is still low.

The activities of the last few months may not be enough to make an argument for the mainstream adoption of Bitcoin. Still, it is undoubtedly enough to start taking cryptocurrency seriously. More importantly, Bitcoin's resurgence has also paved a path for other digital currencies like Ethereum, Litecoin, Dogecoin, and many others.

Best Cryptocurrency You Can Buy in 2021 and Beyond

Cryptocurrencies are currently experiencing their most significant boom period since late 2017, and the world has noticed. Today, investors keep an eye out for the top cryptocurrencies to add more gloss to their portfolios.

Bitcoin remains the most popular cryptocurrency, recently saw its value reach a record high at $63,000. Since then, the value has dipped by more than 50%, but investors are still scampering to take advantage of the current window to buy as many Bitcoin units as possible before the price shoots up again.

Over the past few months, cryptocurrency prices have generally come down from their highs after U.S. President Joe Biden's plans to increase capital gains taxes forced some investors to sell off their holdings. However, this had little impact on the positive outlook of financial services towards cryptocurrency.

In a statement issued by Visa in March, the company revealed that it would allow USDC Stablecoin to make transactions. Earlier in May, the Gemini cryptocurrency exchanges also broke the news of its partnership with MasterCard to launch a reward-based credit card. The idea being to allow users to earn rewards in the form of cryptocurrencies for every transaction completed.

In the same vein, investment banking juggernauts JP Morgan also rolled out plans to launch a managed Bitcoin fund for its customers. It is not just Bitcoin dominating the financial news and gaining widespread acceptance from merchants. The meme crypto that went viral on social media, Dogecoin, has also been accepted by merchants like The Kessler Collection luxury hotel chain, NewEgg, and the Dallas Mavericks NBA team.

With more businesses projected to embrace cryptocurrency as a means of payment in the coming months, there is no better time to invest in cryptocurrencies per your budget. From the most talked-about cryptocurrencies to lesser-known digital currencies, below are a selection of the coins you should consider if you are serious about being a part of the crypto community in 2021. (Note that I have deliberately omitted Bitcoin from the list because I have discussed it extensively throughout this book).

1. Ethereum

You may think only Bitcoin is having a fantastic year, but that is probably because you have not been keeping track of the progress of other cryptocurrencies like Ethereum. Thanks to a combination of factors, including an improved update to its underlying network and a general push for cryptocurrencies, the world's second-largest crypto by market capitalization is on the rise.

To say ether is having a great year would be a massive understatement. Earlier in May, ether's value reached an all-time high when it surpassed $3,430. And crypto experts strongly believe that the year still holds much promise for virtual currency.

Ether has undoubtedly come a long way and fully deserves all the positive attention it has received lately. Ethereum is a software platform that uses blockchain technology, where users can exchange cryptocurrency called ether. It was first proposed by its founder Vitalik Buterin in 2013 and finally launched in 2015. Thanks to the latest surge in the price of ether, Buterin has now joined the billionaires club — with one of his virtual wallets holding ether worth over $1.1bn.

However, the most intriguing thing about ether's recent rise is how it has managed to move independently of the flagship cryptocurrency, Bitcoin, over the last few months. For quite some time, the altcoins have been heavily dependent on whatever happens to

Bitcoin before they experience any sort of movement.

The story is not any different for ether, as it seemed to be inextricably linked to Bitcoin in the past — a selloff for Bitcoin usually resulted in an inevitable knock on the prices of the altcoins, including ether. However, recent showings by ether seem to point at a successful decoupling.

Much of that success achieved by ether can be put down to the progress made by Ethereum over the past couple of months. The platform has made an impressive 500% gains this year, and with new upgrades being introduced to improve the system, including the Berlin hard fork and London hard fork, there is more growth install for ether.

2. Dogecoin

It is a cryptocurrency based on the famous "Doge" internet meme, which features a Shiba Inu dog. It was created in 2013 by two software engineers from IBM and Adobe with the original intent of being a lighthearted cryptocurrency. While the public image of the coin still evokes fun and laughter in many ways, the financial numbers it has racked up in the last couple of months have forced investors to start taking it more seriously.

Since the start of the year, Dogecoin has experienced a surge of more than 14,000%, putting its market capitalization above $84bn — equalling the annual economic output of Sri Lanka. Despite these outrageous numbers, Dogecoin's price still angles at less than a dollar due to its more extensive circulation. There are currently 129 billion Dogecoins in circulation compared to Bitcoin's 21 million market cap.

Meanwhile, Dogecoin has caught on several supporters over the years, including famous faces like Tesla founder Elon Musk, legendary rapper Snoop Dogg and the Kiss bassist Gene Simmons. Musk, in particular, has periodically showcased his support for Dogecoin on Twitter, and his influence came to play as the value of the digital currency spiked by more than 40% to reach $0.68 against the dollar, ahead of Musk's Saturday Night Live appearance at the beginning of May.

Also known as the Dogefather, Musk did not disappoint as he reeled out several Doge-related jokes during his performance as host of SNL. Even though the price of Doge fell immediately after Musk's appearance, the coin's popularity continues to soar, and crypto experts expect it to pick up soon enough.

3. Litecoin

Litecoin may have been created based on the Bitcoin protocol, but it provides many unavailable functions in Bitcoin. The most significant advantage that Litecoin offers over Bitcoin is that it is cheaper and faster — especially when it comes to small transactions such as paying for a cup of coffee or dinner at a restaurant.

Litecoin's compatibility for everyday use makes it a desirable option for anybody and everybody. Additionally, Litecoin is also very easy to use, which offers it a much more realistic push for mainstream adoption than other altcoins.

In that regard, Litecoin is already enjoying massive success — thanks to its inclusion as a means of payment in Venezuela's mainstream international payments system. As a result of Litecoin's partnership with Renesas remittance platform, foreigners can now send the coin to their family and friends in Venezuela. They receive Bolivars in their bank account via remesas.

On the market front, Litecoin's price has been through several ups and downs since its launch in 2011. Its price started at $3 and has gone through several bubble cycles but remains one of the most popular cryptocurrencies in the market.

Following a very remarkable 2020 that saw the Litecoin value go up by more than 140%, experts opine that Litecoin's potential is very high. With the price of Litecoin currently hovering around $175, there is real optimism amongst its supporters that it could break it's all-time high of $370 before the end of the year. In a nutshell, the verdict on Litecoin by most experts is that it is an excellent long-term investment, but the key is to operate within your budget continuously.

The world of financial trading is quite vast and can get very murky if you do not have adequate knowledge and experience. In this world, cryptocurrency is a new area of investment that many people have yet to comprehend fully. And to make things a lot trickier, it brings new sets of problems — like huge volatility and unpredictability — which are not familiar to other conventional currencies.

Investors first began to see cryptocurrency, especially Bitcoin, as an attractive investment vehicle in late 2013 — after BitCoin experienced a massive jump in value from $200 in November 2013 to over $1000 barely a month later. At this point, it is essential to emphasize that volatility does not always yield exceptional gains. As much as it can bring you massive profits, you can also end up losing most of your investment or, worse — all of it.

That is why I advise that as you are taking your first few steps into the cryptocurrency world as an investor, you must proceed with caution. I will leave you with a story of my personal experience, and hopefully, you can pick one of two things from it.

As a young man trying to find my feet as an investor and business owner, I struggled with finding the right amount of funding to push my business projects. I saw an opportunity in the real estate market somewhere in Europe. I quickly had my business plan drawn out and talked to family members and friends to raise the capital I needed to make this big dream a reality. For me, it was no ordinary dream but a very viable business venture that could potentially turn me into a wealthy man — that is, if everything went according to plan.

In my travels, I came across a beautiful remote village somewhere in Europe, which had been abandoned by most of the homeowners for some reason. So, what was left there was just the beautiful scenery — that would have made for a great tourist attraction — and empty houses that cobwebs and dirt had taken over. During my conversations with one of the few remaining locals, I discovered that the places were up for sale at an unbelievable knockdown price. A serious buyer could get the whole village for a good discount. The locals were desperate to do away with the village lifestyle and move to the city to pursue something more extensive.

I was not concerned with what they were eager to do in the city because all I saw at that moment was real estate gold. I immediately made up my mind that I would buy that village and turn it into a beautiful tourist attraction with hotels and other things that would put it on the map and make me a lot of money.

I had some money I had saved up, but it was not even close to buying one-third of the village. But I was not deterred, and I made up my mind that I would take a loan from the bank if it got to that.

After drawing up my business plan, I started my quest for extra funds with my family members and raised some money, but I had only begun to scratch the surface. So I widened my net to extended family members, and sometimes I had to travel many hours to a different state to meet up with these family members to pitch my ideas in the hope of something positive. All my trips ended in futility, and I grew frustrated at the project's lack of progress.

However, I have always been a person who stubbornly pursues whatever I set my mind on. I could see this project yielding so much profit, but nobody else seemed to share my sentiments. I could not even manage to get the loan I needed from the bank to make things worse.

I had grown quite obsessed with making this project happen that it was practically all I talked about at some point. On a fateful day, I made a trip to the bank to "harass" them once again about getting a loan. The lady that attended to me would probably have given me the loan I needed if it meant she would not have to sit and listen to me go about my project for the umpteenth time. Still, unfortunately, it was not within her power — all she could do was to recommend.

While I explained the project to the lady, I had no idea a man was listening to our conversation. I was so engrossed in what I was presenting that I completely missed the fact that there was somebody else in the room. As I left the bank utterly dejected that I had failed with my loan application again, the man approached me and said he would like to invest in the project but would want to see my business plan first and hear more about it.

So we set up a meeting for the next week, and after going through my business plan and listening to me explain the fine details, he once again reiterated his desire to invest in the project, but I had to do one thing first. He said he needed to see that the project was viable, so I should use some of the money I had with me to purchase one of the houses in the village, remodel it and then sell it for more. If I could successfully do those six months from our meeting, he agreed to bankroll the whole project.

That was the best news I had heard in a long time, and it sounded like a very fair deal to me. More importantly, I felt that it should be a task I would complete in less than six months. So off I went, and I quickly bought one of the houses in the village and remodeled it to exquisite taste. Once I was finished with the building, it went straight to the market and stayed there for a whole year without getting a serious offer. During those agonizing 12 months, I began to get more information about the village and why the locals were abandoning their homes to move to the city.

Most of the younger people were leaving the villages for work and opportunities on offer in the city. I realized it would be tough to sell any property in that village for more than the initial price paid for it without developing the neighboring areas. In addition, I came to face the fact that if I were going to create it into a tourist center that would make a lot of profit, it would require a lot more effort than I had envisaged earlier.

I had to abandon that dream and focus more on selling off the house I had bought. After nearly three years on the market, I eventually sold the house to an old couple looking to retire in a peaceful environment. I was glad I could get my money back with a bit of profit, but I was mostly happy with the lessons I had learned from the experience.

In the first place, I did not do enough research about the village before deciding to invest in it. Even though I was pretty new to the real estate market, I just wanted to jump in with so much money because I thought I had found a straightforward way to make a lot of money in one clean swoop. If I had gotten the money I needed from my family members and friends, I would have thrown it into the business and lost most of it. That singular action would have cost me a lot of relationships and given me many sleepless nights. In truth, I may never have recovered from such a setback.

As a newbie investor, my advice to you is to make sure that you take little steps that you can handle if things go south. Never invest what could potentially cripple you financially, and more importantly, do your research before you put your hard-earned money into any cryptocurrency. Finally, take a second and third look when a deal looks too cheap or too good to be true.

Are Cryptocurrencies Legal?

Bitcoin (BTC) was the flagship cryptocurrency. It was well received by people worldwide, which led to the creation of other cryptocurrencies like Ethereum (ETH), Litecoin, Dash, Ripple, and many others. In the years that have followed the launch of Bitcoin, more than 6,000 versions of digital currencies have been created. Now it has become cumbersome to keep track of the lot. More importantly, it is not so easy to know which of them are legal and those that are not.

Remember that Bitcoins, along with other cryptocurrencies, are not issued, backed, or regulated by any central bank — instead, they are created via a computer-based process popularly known as mining. In addition to being completely decentralized, cryptocurrency is a peer-to-peer payment system since it does not have any physical presence or representation. Consequently, it offers a fast and easy way to perform cross-border transactions with little or no exchange rate fees attached. And perhaps the feature of crypto that is most important to this chapter is that it also allows the user's identity to remain hidden.

The fact that cryptocurrencies do not have a regulatory system and cannot be regulated by governments has been the greatest encumbrance of its ascension into the mainstream finance market. Despite the global popularity of cryptocurrencies like Bitcoin, Ethereum, and Dogecoin — coupled with the recent acceptance of some cryptocurrencies as payment options by big name merchants — governments (or countries) are still hesitant to legalize these currencies.

The reluctance of the government to legalize the use of cryptocurrencies is one reason why Bitcoin and the other major digital currencies display high volatility. The uncertainty regarding their future directly impacts their value, making it very difficult to predict for even the most experienced investor.

Apart from the lack of regulation, another problem of cryptocurrency that poses a credible threat to its adoption is the misuse of these virtual currencies and their vulnerability to security attacks from criminally minded hackers. Over the years, regulators have been very vocal about the increasing abuse of digital currencies by criminals for illegal activities. Still, the peculiarities of these currencies have made it impossible for authorities to do much to prevent these crimes.

Since the emergence of cryptocurrency, it has been noted that many illegal activities like money laundering, tax evasion, and terrorist financing have been carried out by criminals using virtual currencies. Back in July 2019, investment banker and former U.S. Treasury Secretary Steven Mnuchin aired his concerns about the misuse of Facebook, Inc.'s patented Libra virtual currency by money launderers and terrorist financiers.

Shortly after announcing the Libra project in June 2019, it faced heavy backlash from policymakers worldwide, who cited concerns over money laundering, data security, and consumer protections. While responding to the claims made by Mnuchin, Facebook

Inc.'s Head of blockchain efforts, David Marcus, revealed that the company had decided to put the launch of Libra on hold until they had "fully addressed regulatory concerns" and gotten the necessary approvals.

Still, the case of Libra is just a one-off as there are still thousands of cryptocurrencies being traded publicly without any form of regulation. This has periodically led to the loss of investment holdings from cyber-attacks, thereby hindering the adoption of cryptocurrencies. For example, in February 2020, crypto exchange platforms — Okex.Com and Bitfinex — were disrupted with Denial of Service attacks. Security breaches of this nature and the continued misuse of cryptocurrencies are fast becoming a significant mitigating factor to this market's general growth and development.

Criminals and terrorists characteristically prefer to deal in cash and hold cash as collateral instead of using financial intermediaries such as banks to avoid compliance regulations and anti-money laundering reporting. In addition, businesses and governments fear that the decentralized and pseudonymous nature

of cryptocurrency transfers makes it easy for criminals to conceal their digital footprints. By extension, their financial activities from law enforcement agencies.

A perfect example of such a scenario was how Bitcoin was used on the web-based, illicit drug market called Silk Road. The combination of Silk Road and a Bitcoin escrow program facilitated over 100,000 unlawful product transactions between January 2011 and October 2013, when the government clamped down on the company and apprehended the individuals running the platform.

Despite all the negativity generated by the unlawful use of virtual currencies, the crypto space continues to expand rapidly because the advantages that it offers its users far outweigh the social expense of increased theft and illegality facilitated by virtual currency. However, regulators remain resolute in their bid to find a lasting solution to these criminal activities — even if it means restricting cryptocurrency exchanges to legislation associated with the tracking of criminal behavior.

Impact of Regulation

Many of the state agencies and Federal commissions in the United States of America and agencies in other countries have notably regulated some applications for cryptocurrency over the years. However, the disparities in the approaches taken by different agencies within the U.S. and other countries across the globe have generated much confusion about the extent to which appropriate authorities can regulate cryptocurrency and blockchain technology.

The absence of government backing and proper regularization across the globe is one of the significant mitigating factors for the adoption of cryptocurrencies by the government. On the side of investors, the crypto space carries enough risks without adequate protection and therefore restrains many investors from investing as much as they would like.

In response to the increased risks associated with the use of these currencies, some regions have outrightly banned cryptocurrency citing its misuse for criminal activities such as terrorism and money laundering. Meanwhile, some countries have made efforts to regulate the crypto space within their region. For example, in March 2020, the Reserve Bank of Zimbabwe revealed its plans to develop a regulatory structure for monitoring companies' operations that trade cryptocurrencies.

Different countries have legal frameworks through which they regulate cryptocurrency. While some countries have enacted policies to either encourage or curb the use of digital currencies, there are no clear-cut policies, while there are a few countries that backed the use of cryptocurrency. Below we take a look at various countries and how they deal with cryptocurrency.

Countries That Are Not Crypto-Friendly

Although Bitcoin has been embraced in many parts of the world, a few countries have chosen to keep their distance due to its decentralized nature. Volatility links to illicit activities like money laundering, drug trafficking, and perceived threat to current monetary systems. In response, some nations have outrightly banned the use of digital currency. In contrast, others have stifled its growth In their region by cutting off any support from the banking and financial system, which are necessary for its trading and use.

- **China**

By early 2018, China had prohibited all activities linked to cryptocurrencies from taking place within its borders. The government also began a massive crackdown on crypto miners and shut down existing domestic cryptocurrency exchanges. In addition, the government also enacted an access ban on all domestic and foreign crypto exchange platforms. According to the ex-governor of the People's Bank of China, Zhou Xiaochuan, explicit instructions have been sent to all the local financial institutions within the country by the regulators that no digital currencies should be recognized as a means of making any retail payment.

- **Russia**

Russia recently shifted from its previous hard stance on digital currencies after signing a new cryptocurrency law. Which lifts the last ban on cryptocurrencies but still imposed strict limitations on its use as any form of monetary currency. This development follows a previous regulatory filing that practically linked all activities involving digital currencies as unlawful and put them under the jurisdiction of anti-money laundering laws.

As per the newly enacted law, cryptocurrencies were allowed in Russia from January 1st, 2021. However, they are not allowed to be used to exchange to acquire any goods or services. The door remains open for more regulation of the crypto space within the country during upcoming sessions. It seems that Russians are allowed to mine, trade cryptocurrencies for other cryptocurrencies on exchanges without fearing any legal repercussions — provided they do not use it as payment for goods and services within the country's borders.

- **Vietnam**

As of today, Vietnamese law does not recognize cryptocurrencies as a legitimate payment method, and neither does it recognize them as an investment or a foreign currency. Also, the Vietnamese government and its State bank have expressly designated Bitcoin, and other digital currencies as illegal and prohibited for trade relationships.

Therefore, any usage, supply, and issuance of cryptocurrencies within the country's borders will be met with strict fines — up to US$8,700 — and jail time.

However, it is not forbidden nor permitted for citizens to possess, trade, and invest in cryptocurrencies; it is only being tolerated pending a review of the existing law.

- **Bolivia, Colombia, and Ecuador El Banco Central de Bolivia**

All have prohibited the use of all cryptocurrencies within the country. Similarly, Columbia has also banned crypto use or investment. Finally, Bitcoin and similar cryptocurrencies were outlawed in Ecuador, thanks to a majority vote during a national assembly session. Other countries where cryptocurrencies are banned include

- **Algeria**
- **Ecuador**
- **Bolivia**
- **Bangladesh**
- **Nepal**
- **Macedonia**

Countries That Are Crypto-Friendly

Cryptocurrency ensures that users remain anonymous and can perform transactions with other crypto users anywhere and anytime across the world — making it very appealing to terror organizations and criminals. These criminals use cryptocurrency such as Bitcoin to buy or sell illicit goods like weapons or drugs, and the transactions are impossible to link back to them or their organization.

Today, most countries are still determining the legality of the various cryptocurrencies and prefer to take an observatory approach instead. Meanwhile, some other nations have indirectly approved the legal use of digital currencies by deliberately installing some regulatory oversight. Still, no country would accept any of the cryptocurrencies as a direct substitute for its legal tender.

- **The United States**

The U.S. government has unarguably been more open and positive about cryptocurrencies than its counterparts across the globe. This has placed the United States ahead of other countries regarding the adoption of cryptocurrencies and their usage. The U.S. government has even gone a step further by classifying Cryptocurrencies as MSB (Money Services Business) — with clear instructions passed to several government bodies that crypto-related transactions must be carried out through proper legal channels, as there is a presence of digital currencies in the U.S. derivatives market.

Consequently, investors within the U.S. borders have the option of purchasing Bitcoin along with other 45 virtual assets across the nation. It is important to note that cryptocurrency has been classified by the country's Financial Crimes Enforcement Network (FinCEN) as "money transmitters," so a unique set of niche laws binds them. In like manner, the Internal Revenue Service (IRS) has also categorized crypto assets as those with property and value, and so cryptocurrencies are taxable commodities in the U.S. Moreover, the laws regarding cryptocurrency are uniquely different in every state across America. At the national level, regulators also have varying opinions on the methods used to handle cryptocurrencies.

For example, while the Commodity Futures Trading Commission (CFTC) categorized them as commodities (thereby allowing users to trade crypto derivatives publicly), the Securities and Exchange Commission (SEC) classes digital currencies to be securities. The United States government has been proactive about its handling of cryptocurrency, which is evident in the continuous upgrade of policies associated with the crypto space. More recently, the U.S. Congress released a Joint Economic Report (JER), which hinted that the country would adopt a more streamlined regulatory approach to crypto within the next 12 months.

- **Canada**

Canada shares many similarities to the U.S., and they have continued this trend with their handling of cryptocurrencies. The country has been quite positive about approving cryptocurrencies and is currently home to several established crypto companies and startups. Furthermore, Canada can be said to be way ahead of most countries when it comes to the adoption of cryptocurrencies, as it already sees and sees digital currencies as a viable alternative tool for payment in the future. Cryptocurrencies are categorized as a commodity in Canada — meaning all transactions completed using cryptocurrency within the country are legitimately tagged as a barter trade. Therefore, any income drawn from cryptocurrencies is basically "business income.".

More importantly, the Canadian government has taken active steps to protect crypto users within its territory and also wants to ensure strict Anti Money Laundering laws govern the use of cryptocurrencies.

Consequently, the country's legal system mandates that any firms that deal with digital currencies must be registered with the Financial Transactions and Reports Analysis Centre of Canada (FINTRAC).

Moreover, local banks cannot open or service the client's accounts to transact with digital currencies (i.e., if they are yet to register with FINTRAC).

- **United Kingdom**

The U.K. ranks up there when it comes to crypto adoption and innovation. The use of digital currencies has never been prohibited across the country, but they are still some way off being considered to be legal tender. In addition, no value-added tax (VAT) is attached to the purchase of various cryptocurrencies within the country. Instead, a surcharge is placed on goods or services obtained while using Bitcoin or other similar digital currencies as a means of payment.

Meanwhile, crypto investors within the U.K. are subject to capital gains tax, whether their crypto assets incur profits or losses. Also, CryptoUK, a self-regulatory trade association, is pushing to enhance the U.K.'s existing industry standards (relating to Bitcoin) by implementing a code of conduct that encompasses several niche provisions linked to individual privacy data security and anti-money laundering.

- **Australia**

Over the years, the Reserve Bank of Australia has always appeared to be open-minded towards the crypto industry. The regulatory body has also stated publicly that it does not stop people from making use of cryptocurrencies. In 2017, the Australian government announced that Bitcoin would be treated like traditional currency and will not be subject to double taxation.

- **France**

A court ruling regarding the use of cryptocurrency in the country offered the companies which handle cryptocurrency or offer crypto-related services legal certainty to run their operation in the country. Before this ruling, the country passed a bill geared towards putting in place a new legal framework to oversee cryptocurrency operations like Initial Coin Offerings (ICOs) throughout the country.

In addition, crypto-related companies are expected to adhere to capital requirements and consumer protection standards voluntarily. They are also required to pay tax in the country, which guarantees approval from the regulator.

- **Germany**

Germany is also considered to be quite open about digital currencies. The German Federal Financial Supervisory Authority (BaFin) categorizes cryptocurrencies as "units of account" that may be used as a means of payment. However, individuals, groups, or companies that operate token purchases (especially for commercial reasons) must obtain a permit from the regulatory body in advance. Moreover, BaFin has authorized a case-by-case vetting for companies interested in setting up an Initial Coin Offering (ICO), which suggests that it has an open mind towards such a developing fundraising system.

Since the beginning of the year 2020, commercial banks and other traditional financial institutions within the country were authorized to operate digital currencies like bitcoin on behalf of their clients after modifications were accepted by Berlin to ascent Europe's anti-money laundering regulations into national law.

- **Japan**

Over the years, Japan has earned a reputation as one of the fastest developing technology markets in the world. So it was only a matter of time for Japan to get on board with crypto by legalizing its use. The popular Asian country's government has established a unique PSA (Payment Services Act) based structure that permits some cryptocurrencies and selected exchanges to be employed as a tool for payment and trading. Today, Japan is now widely regarded as the hub for cryptocurrency trading/exchange in Asia. The increasing popularity of Bitcoin and other cryptocurrencies has helped it to gain wider acceptance across the globe.

The impact of the soaring popularity of the crypto industry has been so profound that many countries that had previously banned cryptocurrencies have now shifted their stance and legalized it. A typical example of such is India, which recently lifted its ban, thereby legalizing the use of cryptocurrency within the country. The Indian government has made additional provisions to keep pace with the trend and placed a tax on digital currency trading.

Other countries that have legalized cryptocurrency include: Namibia, Nigeria, Morocco, South Africa, Mexico, Costa Rica, Trinidad and Tobago, Brazil, Nicaragua, Lebanon, Turkey, Saudi Arabia, UAE, Iran, Cyprus, Palestine, Hong Kong, Taiwan, South Korea, Malaysia, Cambodia, Philippines, Indonesia, Singapore, Croatia, Holland, Poland, Austria, Slovenia, Slovakia, Switzerland, New Zealand, Belgium, Ireland, Greece, Bulgaria, Luxembourg, Italy, Malta, Bosnia and Herzegovina, Spain, Ireland, Portugal, Iceland, Norway, Denmark, and Ukraine.

While many countries are still in the process of constructing an economic framework for digital currency, some countries have already developed systems that require the crypto service providers to be licensed by the relevant local regulatory bodies. With cryptocurrency projected for more growth in the coming years, it is expected that those countries that still have bans on all crypto-related activities would ditch their ban and embrace the use of virtual currencies.

How Do I Protect Myself From Scammers?

The year 2020 was a very defining one for many individuals and families across the globe as the novel coronavirus pandemic forced cities into lockdown, thereby crippling economic activities. Barely halfway through the year and almost everyone could testify that their lives had gone through some significant changes — not just personally but also in business.

Many businesses were shut down, shows were canceled, the hospitality industry took a great hit, and the entertainment world also suffered due to the postponement or outright cancellation of programs. However, the finance and economic sector were the most affected by the effects of the highly contagious COVID-19, with more than 40 million people filing for unemployment in the U.S. alone. But through the darkness brought about by the global pandemic, a path shone through for cryptocurrency.

Despite many people losing their income and employment due to the shutdown of economic activities, the pandemic inspired drove mainstream adoption of digital currencies in a way that had never been seen in the decade-long existence of the flagship cryptocurrency, Bitcoin. From March 2020 to April 2021, Bitcoin's performance completely crushed traditional stock markets, and experts are still predicting further gains for the cryptocurrency this year, despite a recent dip in price.

Still, if there is one thing we have learned over the years, the crypto space is a complex world characterized by guidelines and techniques that are difficult for the uninitiated to comprehend. Over the last 12 months, Bitcoin has outperformed some "safe investments" like natural oil and gas and even the U.S. Dollar. Thanks to this remarkable feat, crypto proved its value to many investors, especially as a hedge or safe haven in a market that is mostly unpredictable. However, the major drawback of the crypto space is its volatility, as even the most skilled economists find it difficult to forecast the long-term performance of Bitcoin, let alone more than 5,000 other digital currencies that are active in the market.

Undoubtedly, investing in cryptocurrency has the potential to bring massive gains. I have personally enjoyed such gains from my investments in Bitcoin, Ripple, Ethereum, and other coins, as an early adopter who saw their future potential when they first hit the market. My crypto adventure thus far has given me an increased income and afforded me more time to indulge in activities I enjoy. Indeed, several benefits come with a choice to invest in crypto. You must understand that there is still a lot more for you to learn at this point and even in the future.

Over the past few months alone, the prices of many of these virtual assets have soared. In addition, there is now an exceedingly abundant number of coins to evaluate before you can confidently bet on (or against) them. As if the problems were not enough already, it has become more challenging to remain patient and compete with alternative, less volatile investment opportunities (such as the conventional stock market). That being said, I must emphasize that investing in cryptocurrency comes with a very high level of risk. As a newbie investor, there are several potential hazards that you must vigilantly be on the lookout for. But the work does not just stop paying attention; you must learn to protect yourself as a newbie investor trying to make a new income with cryptocurrency.

Below, we will talk about ways you can protect yourself in risky crypto space. But before that, I would first like to explain why you should reconsider your decision to invest in cryptocurrency.

The Market is Volatile

Over the last few months, the price of Bitcoin has experienced massive fluctuation in price, and it is not even remotely close to the most volatile digital currency in the crypto world. The prices of these assets are rapidly going up and down, so if you purchase them at the wrong time, there is a likelihood of you losing a huge sum of money fast.

There is So Much to Understand

Many people buy cryptocurrency without fully understanding it but hoping that they would make money from it. The fact is that it is quite tempting to travel down that road since they have seen others do the same and make a lot of money. However, investing in something based on technology as complex as the blockchain without proper research is quite risky. A major reason for the volatility displayed by these coins is that most people do not have an idea of how much they should be worth.

The Adoption Timeline is Ambiguous

Even though we have seen a recent increase in the number of businesses that are beginning to accept crypto payment and a rise in the number of active blockchain companies, yet the timeline for widespread adoption of cryptocurrency is mostly speculative.

As it remains difficult to make a precise argument for the point in time that these coins will be completely accepted into the mainstream market, all current investment in cryptocurrency is at best speculative. This assertion is backed by the fact that there are low odds placed on the capacity of all the current coins to survive and thrive in the future.

Ability to Survive and Thrive

Based on the current popularity of cryptocurrency and how many big companies have been joining the crypto space. It is fair to say that a handful of the existing digital currencies will survive and thrive, but how much each of them will be worth. The offerings that will be worth something special are another topic entirely. The answers to these questions can only be unearthed by having a deep understanding of blockchain technology and how society works.

Yes, sociology is a core ingredient of the whole setup because the success of cryptocurrency is highly dependent on governments, societies, and the ways by which groups of people adopt them. It is quite easy to conclude that because an application presents many advantages to people, they should easily gravitate towards adopting it.

However, that is not how society works. Every individual thinks and behaves differently from the next person. These differences are further highlighted across geographical regions — making it difficult to put an exact time for the general adoption of these coins across the globe.

The Market Will Crash at Some Point

From what we have seen so far, the high volatility displayed by cryptocurrencies over the years can point to a definite crash of the crypto market at some point in the future. While these might not happen with all the coins and could occur anytime from now, the fact remains that high odds support these possibilities. I know the same can be said about the stock markets. The key disparity is that the rapid and unprecedented success that has been associated with cryptocurrency prices over the last 12 months has set it up for a big-impact fall.

The fact remains that stocks are less likely to be as heavily overvalued as digital currencies. You are only human to want to jump into the crypto space after seeing the countless number of people that have heavily profited from the recent surge in prices of various coins. However, I must warn you again that chasing crypto is a risky business, and you must prepare yourself for it if you remain persistent about investing in this space. The truth is that the high prices are difficult to explain or justify, making it very unpredictable.

Large Profits Can No Longer Be Made on the Popular Coins

Over the past year, many people have made ten times the money they invested in popular coins like Bitcoin and Ethereum. With the current values of these coins, I think it is pretty safe to say that you should not expect that same level of yield from your investment at this point. With every passing day, the odds that Bitcoin's value would increase by even 100% is growing less likely.

Though there is still the potential of making great gains from the less popular coins. However, the problem here is that there is no guarantee that those coins will turn up great profits. In addition, some people are doing everything they can to pull the values of these coins so they can make quick profits. However, the problem here is that anything that is not made to go through a process tends to fall quickly as it rises.

For these people, it is all about pumping the values of these coins by exciting them up and investing a lot of money in them before making a quick cash-out by selling their assets shortly after they accomplish their goals. Their selfish actions put many innocent people at risk of making huge losses, which is why you must have a deep understanding of the market so you can be rightly guided in making a decent choice for your investment portfolio.

Undoubtedly, there are many risks that you will come to face if you decide to go ahead with investing in cryptocurrency. If you are still hellbent on crypto, apart from doing your private research about the crypto space and the coin you want to purchase, you must also take some necessary steps to protect yourself. Also, from an investment point of view, you should try to scatter your investment portfolio across a wide range of assets. However, if you are determined to limit your investment to only the crypto space, do so with your eyes open to the enormous risk before you.

What your actions mean is that You are betting heavily on the chances of cryptocurrency succeeding. While the current trends point to that statement being true (and I am a firm believer), if the unexpected happens, you will most likely find yourself in a tight situation. My advice is to try as much as possible to diversify your investment across different coins instead of putting all your money in just one coin. The key thing you must take from all of these is that when it comes to cryptocurrency, make sure all your decisions are supported by adequate information.

If you will take my advice and invest in more than one coin, make sure you do a thorough investigation before jumping into the market. It is your money, and so you must be the most serious about protecting it. Still, the best bet would be for you to diversify with non-crypto assets as you invest in digital currencies. Again, putting all your hard-earned money into the blockchain could bring you huge gains as much as it could bring you losses.

Therefore, spreading your money across various asset types will ensure you remain financially stable if there is a crash in cryptocurrency. This is just one way you can protect yourself from the volatility that is common to cryptocurrencies. Now, I will discuss other ways to protect yourself from other risks associated with cryptocurrency, including security. Here are some ways you can do just that:

Secure Your Computer and Data

As I have discussed earlier in this book, cryptocurrency is very vulnerable to attacks from hackers, so you must ensure to protect yourself at all costs. Ensure you always update your antivirus software to the latest versions and never give out your data online when you begin to store or invest in cryptocurrency.

Any loose handling of your data online can leave you exposed to hackers who specialize in emptying crypto wallets. More importantly, if you decide to store cryptocurrency, make sure you have multiple wallets to keep your holdings. For maximum safety, you can even keep your wallets offline, using a physical tool such as a USB.

Do a Thorough Investigation Before Investing in ICOs

Lately, ICOs or Initial Coin Offerings have emerged as a popular means which cryptocurrencies raise funds from the public. However, like everything that can be exploited, they have also become an easy way to dupe vulnerable people for their hard- earned money. Recently, the financial regulator warned crypto users about what it described as "these very high risk, speculative investments." Going further, the regulator also warned about how there is little to no consumer protection and a high propensity for fraud and high volatility.

While the FCA regulates some ICOs, it must be noted that this only happens on a case-by-case basis, depending on their structuring.

The FCA clearly warns potential investors to investigate any ICO before investing their money thoroughly. A spokesman for the FCA explicitly advises customers to only invest in an ICO project if they have adequate experience as an investor and are confident in the realness of the ICO project itself. Moreover, to save yourself from unnecessary headaches, only consider dealing with regulated ICOs.

Build Immunity Against FOMO

In the investment world, the fear of missing out (FOMO) has cost many people their hard-earned money. And this has become more rampant today due to the boom that has become associated with cryptocurrency. However, because your neighbor or friend made so many profits on a particular cryptocurrency does not necessarily mean you will make gains too.

I have realized that when there is so much buzz about a particular investment, it is already too late to jump in for the same maximum profits. Never substitute proper research, understand what you are getting into, and objective analysis of loss potential with FOMO — unless you are ready for a fall.

Know Your Leverage

This is for the advantage of those who may decide to invest in digital currencies through a contract for difference (CFD) or spread bet (FSB). When you invest using any of these platforms, you must understand that your losses and profits can be magnified via leverage. So it is your responsibility to understand the leverage attached to your investments and whether it could translate to you losing more than your initial investment. It is pertinent that you trade with a company that offers CFDs regulated by the FCA for your benefit.

Who Owns a Crypto Company?

Now that we are past all the negativity and risk surrounding cryptocurrency and you are still determined about making money from the crypto space, you need to know how to get this party started. Anyone looking to get into the crypto space will need to open up a wallet on a cryptocurrency exchange.

What is a Cryptocurrency Exchange?

It can be described as a business that allows its users to trade digital currencies for other assets like traditional fiat money or other cryptocurrencies. Note that exchanges may choose to accept wire transfers, credit card payments, or other means of payment in exchange for cryptocurrencies. Typically, there are no restrictions to who may or may not own a cryptocurrency exchange — you have to meet certain conditions.

To start your cryptocurrency exchange, there are certain things you will need to consider, including what the internal architecture of the exchange should look like and, more importantly, where you can get the software to power your exchange. Starting a cryptocurrency exchange involves six steps and, of course, a sizable capital. I will quickly list these steps for you to have a better understanding of everything related to cryptocurrency. After all, that is the main inspiration behind this book — to open your eyes to the limitless possibilities in the cryptocurrency space. So here we go!

1. Determine the location where you would like to do business. Make sure your decision is based on a good

market survey and caters to a good population of people.

2. Take it upon yourself to learn about the regulations in that area, to prevent problems in the future
3. Join forces with a payment processor or bank to help you with effective cash payments to your user's
4. Setup liquidity and transaction history on the exchange
5. Put in place best security practices to protect the holdings of your users
6. Finally, make sure you put in place a healthy customer support system.

For a newbie investor, jumping the queue and moving straight to establishing your cryptocurrency exchange is more like financial suicide. Apart from getting a deep understanding of the crypto space, you will also need the right business acumen to effectively manage the company because you will be operating on a much bigger scale. At this point, you will not just have your assets to ponder about, but the hard-earned money of thousands of people would be under your care. Unless you are just deliberately looking to find some trouble, I would strongly advise that you stick to investing in cryptocurrency by opening up a wallet in one of the reputable crypto exchange companies. That should not take you more than a few minutes once you have settled on the most suitable exchange platform for your needs.

At first glance, this may seem like quite an easy task, but it is anything but that. Several trading platforms exist in the market, and every one of them offers something different. To help you with coming to the right decision, here are some things you need to put into perspective before picking a particular crypto exchange platform.

How Secure is Your Fund?

This is the first thing you must verify before you put your money into any crypto exchange platform. If you will be depositing a large sum of money, it is your responsibility to make sure that there is some guarantee that your money is secure. Over the years, we have seen several cases of large cryptocurrency platforms that went bankrupt and took their users' money with them. I assure you that it is more painful when you lose a large sum of money, and you can trace it back to your negligence.

Let us prevent that by taking adequate time to investigate what safeguards have been put in place by a particular platform, so you can ascertain whether or not they are suitable for your needs. Most times, this type of information is likely to be posted on the cryptocurrency exchange platform's website. Taking time to read over this information thoroughly is crucial before you put your money into the platform.

How Many Cryptocurrencies are Available?

Before deciding on any cryptocurrency exchange, you must find out how many different digital currencies they deal with. With More than 1,300 versions of cryptocurrency available in the market, you will have to do some thorough research to arrive at the crypto option to invest your money. Most of the cryptocurrencies available in the market are peer-to-peer, which means that they will not be available on most exchanges. The higher percentage of the exchanges out there will only present you with a handful of investment options.

Making sure you take your time to go through which cryptocurrency options most appeal to you is very important to the success of your investment. Once you have obtained this information, you will be better equipped to settle on the best exchange for your needs. Trying to rush decisions as crucial as this will do you more harm than good and may eventually lead to losing a lot of money in the future.

Compare Transaction Fees

Most cryptocurrency exchange companies make most of their earnings from transaction fees charged. Every time you complete a transaction, you are charged a fee by the exchange. This is why it is pertinent that you find out what type of fees are charged by an exchange platform before you invest your money. It will be very counterproductive if all the profits you are supposed to earn go towards paying off these fees. Make sure you contact each of the crypto exchange platforms you have your eyes on and enquire about their transaction fees. By doing so, you will be able to compare the fees charged by each company and arrive at the cheapest and most profitable offer for you.

Ease of Use

As a newbie in the crypto space, it is essential that you find a cryptocurrency trading platform that is easy to navigate. Attempting to trade on a platform that is difficult to operate will frustrate your effort and most likely lead to many avoidable errors.

Please take advantage of the free trials offered by most of these platforms to test how easy they are to operate and the types of currencies they have on offer.

In addition, it can be helpful to seek advice on which type of cryptocurrency exchange platform to use from an experienced cryptocurrency investor. These experts can help you avoid a lot of errors that are common to newbie crypto traders. Thankfully, that is what I am here to help you with through this book.

When it comes to cryptocurrency, most professionals prefer to point their clients in the right direction and leave the bulk of decision-making. This is the majority due to the volatility of the crypto space and to make clients completely responsible for all of their financial choices.

Even though I have carefully provided you with all the facts, you will need to start your cryptocurrency portfolio. I have still emphasized the importance of doing your research so that you can settle for situations that are within your control. That being said, I have shortlisted three of the best cryptocurrency exchange platforms out there. You can learn about them and take some time to do your research on them before you finally put your money into a particular platform.

1. Coinbase

It was founded in 2012. It is one of the most reliable cryptocurrency exchanges in the U.S., with over 50 cryptocurrency coins, including Bitcoin, Dogecoin, and Ripple, available for trading on the platform. Coinbase is hands-down the most widely used crypto exchange in the U.S., and it operates legally in over 40 states and territories across the country. Apart from being fully licensed and regulated, Coinbase has mostly steered clear of any controversies, especially when it comes to fraud which is a common theme among crypto exchanges. The platform is also very user-friendly and does not require too much expertise to navigate through it.

Features

- Coinbase Pro advanced account
- Coinbase Earn rewards

- User-controlled storage
- Trading tools
- Staking
- Stablecoin

Cons

- It includes high transaction fees and trading fees in the non-pro version
- 0.50% for buy/sell transactions
- Transaction fee ranges between $0.99 to $2.99
- About 0.50% for the pro version.

2. Binance

Binance was founded in 2017 and has a strong focus on alt- coins trading. The platform provides users with over 100 different trading pairs between different digital currencies and several fiat- crypto pairs. Binance is one of the few cryptocurrency exchange platforms with its crypto coin called Binance Coin and is ranked up there alongside the biggest global exchanges, with thousands of exchanges confirmed per day. You can also buy any cryptocurrency of your choice using several payment methods, including debit and credit cards or through GBP or EUR purchases.

Features

- Over 150 different altcoins available on the platform
- Automated recurring buys
- Advanced charting
- Over-the-counter trading

Cons

- It is not beginner-friendly
- It is not available in some U.S. states

Fees

- 0.1% charged as spot trading fee
- 0.5% instant fee to buy/sell
- 4.5% fee deposits on U.S. debit cards

3. Bisq

Unlike traditional banking accounts with physical and geographical representation, digital currencies like Bitcoin were designed to be accessible from any location across the world. Bisq is a decentralized exchange that makes it possible for people from a less-developed banking system to access Bitcoin. The popular exchange offers decentralized peer-to-peer Bitcoin and other cryptocurrencies to download the software that rarely fails.

Unlike other crypto exchanges, bisque does not have a registration process and is readily available to anyone who owns a smartphone or tablet. It is most suitable for anybody looking for a very private platform that prioritizes user anonymity.

Features

- Decentralized platform
- Several payment options available
- Existence of mobile app for Android and iOS systems

Cons

- Generally slow transaction speed

- Fussy active trading
- Low trading volumes

There are several other cryptocurrency exchange platforms currently in operation, but the exchanges above have proven to be the safest and most reliable platforms over the years. While you will do no wrong by investing your money in any of the platforms listed above, there is still so much information that can be gotten try acquired gotten sounds harsh to read about them and all you need to do is visit their official website. Investing in cryptocurrency is a precarious business, so you must make sure you cover every possible angle. Many people treat it as an easy way of making money. That is why there have been many casualties for every success story in the crypto space who have lost their hard-earned money due to mistakes that could have been avoided if they armed themselves with the right information.

Are Cryptocurrencies A Good Investment?

Since the turn of the century, several groundbreaking technological advances have brought about remarkable changes in our everyday lives. From the way we communicate to our friends and families to the way we perform even the most basic chores at home — one way or the other, technology has touched our lives. We can feel the effects of technology in our healthcare system, agriculture sector, manufacturing, and even Hollywood recently got a touch of technology with the introduction of computer-generated imagery (CGI). Which has been hugely successful and used in many blockbuster movies, including *Jungle Book, Inception, War of the Worlds, King Kong, Rise of the Planet of the Apes, Avatar,* and many more.

The novel coronavirus pandemic also showed the world that a lot could be done from working at home. Many companies are now exploring the possibilities of having some of their staff work remotely because it helps them save a lot of money. This would have been used to take care of the operational cost of the day-to- day running of their business. Similarly, many merchants have seen a spike in the number of online orders they receive for different services since the pandemic forced major cities across the globe into a lockdown.

Now more people realize they do not have to leave their homes to get so many things, including food and even groceries. At the thick of the second wave of the novel coronavirus pandemic, the United States conducted the 2020 Presidential elections in November. We must remember that the technology of the mail-in ballots was crucial to ensuring President Joe Biden's victory at the polls. So if we can accept the wholesale changes that technology has brought in virtually all facets of human existence, why is it so unimaginable that technology will play a crucial role with the emergence of cryptocurrency as the future of money? For so long, there has been an increasing dissatisfaction from customers about the services provided by the traditional banking institutions. After the global financial crisis, this disillusion came to a head in 2008 and inadvertently gave Bitcoin a soft landing in 2009.

Since then, Bitcoin has grown massively, and its success opened the floor for the launch of several other cryptocurrencies. Since the 2008 financial crisis, the traditional banking institutions have fought hard to restore the public's trust in them. The novel coronavirus outbreak did them no favors as it showed the world for the second time in 12 years why it needed cryptocurrency. While the global economic landscape succumbed to the crippling effects of the lockdown — with the values of fiat currencies tumbling down — Bitcoin enjoyed a massive surge in value from March 2020 that continued until April this year.

It has not only been a Bitcoin show, but other cryptocurrencies have also joined the party — making it an exciting 12 months for the crypto world. Since the beginning of the year, Bitcoin has enjoyed a price increase of nearly 90%. Meanwhile, Ethereum has experienced a price surge of about 435%, and the most impressive growth has come from Dogecoin with a whopping price increase of 7,800% within the same period. With such incredible numbers, everyone's focus, including the media, has shifted to cryptocurrency, and not a day goes by without one or more of the available digital currencies being featured in the news.

Several big-name companies have started accepting cryptocurrency as a means of payment for their services. Thereby paving the way to mainstream adoption of cryptocurrencies. While the crypto space may still be somehow off that mark, the current trend points to it happening at some point in the future. Countries like India and Russia, which previously maintained a strong stance against the use of digital currencies within their territories, have now softened their stance. It has been predicted that many other countries that also placed bans on cryptocurrency would follow suit in the coming years.

While there is no certainty as to when Bitcoin and other cryptocurrencies would enjoy widespread acceptance worldwide, there is still much enthusiasm surrounding the crypto space. More importantly, cryptocurrencies like Bitcoin have potentially reached a level of popularity and acceptance that it would be nearly impossible for it just to pack up and disappear into oblivion. That being said, many experts opine that cryptocurrency is here to stay, and I strongly agree with them.

Deutsche Bank seems to agree with the views that cryptocurrency will be around for a long time to come. While admitting that the current money system is weak, the Deutsche Bank made the bold prediction that by 2030, the number of crypto users would have risen to about 200 million. In the report titled "Imagine 2030," the Deutsche Bank implies that cryptocurrency could eventually replace the regular fiat currencies as the demand for anonymity and a more decentralized payment model continues to rise. At this point, I think we are beyond asking whether you are interested in investing in cryptocurrency.

While there is so much buzz and excitement surrounding the potential of cryptocurrency, you must remember that they are still very volatile. As such, there must be a clear distinction when you finally decide to invest in it. My advice is to treat your "investment" not any different from how you would treat any other highly volatile venture. In plain terms, you must recognize the fact that you risk losing some of your investment, if not all of it.

One of the factors that make cryptocurrencies very volatile is that they have no intrinsic value, apart from what a buyer bids on them at any point in time. As a result, digital currencies are prone to major price swings, which inadvertently puts an investor at high risk of loss. A typical example of this massive price swing was recorded on

April 11, 2013, when Bitcoin dipped in value from $260 to about $130 within six hours. More recently, Bitcoin dipped in value by over 40% after experiencing an impressive surge in value that saw its peak at $63,000 in April. If you do not have the heart to deal with such volatility, you do not have any business meddling with the crypto market.

The constant price surges associated with cryptocurrencies, especially Bitcoin, have sparked a raging debate about cryptocurrencies' future holds. The question that continues to dominate most of the conversations surrounding Bitcoin and alt-coins is whether these alternative currencies will eventually replace traditional fiat currencies like dollars and euros? Or will cryptocurrencies eventually succumb to the pressures surrounding an upgrade to the mainstream and fade out into obscurity?

For now, it is quite clear to see that the traditional fiat currencies are still what most people rely on when it comes to moving money or performing transactions. This is because there is still some amount of trust in the system that controls the fiat currencies, but most people trust and believe in the currencies. While the United States has been open about cryptocurrency and probably records the greatest daily use of digital currencies — it would still take some time before Americans will completely lose faith in the dollar.

Despite this slight setback, the crypto space has gained ground over the last few years. The evidence of this growth can be seen in almost every sphere of our lives. For example, before 2017, it was tough for cryptocurrency to be the subject of mainstream media coverage. However, that story has changed with almost every important news outlet covering every movement made by Bitcoin in the market. From Forbes to Fidelity, everyone seems eager to give their opinion on the emergence of Bitcoin and other cryptocurrencies as a credible replacement for the traditional fiat currencies. So what does the future hold for cryptocurrency? You need to understand cryptocurrency because the incessant heavy price swings would continue for the foreseeable future until the price of the most popular digital currency, Bitcoin, can stabilize.

While most analysts believe in Bitcoin's short-term ability to bounce back after suffering its regular price fluctuations, critics see it as a major drawback for its general ascension into mainstream finance. I feel the constant price surges are doing cryptocurrencies a solid favor in that it is making them a lot stronger and rugged. For a currency to succeed, it needs to have been tested over time, and nothing can beat the constant price shocks suffered by these digital currencies.

People still choose to invest their money in cryptocurrency, even though it has proven to be unstable, which is a testament to the current strength wielded by these coins. To further support the credibility of cryptocurrency, some analysts predict a significant change in crypto is imminent as institutional money makes its way into the market. Another big plus for the crypto space is the possibility that cryptocurrency may be floated on Nasdaq — a move that is likely to add more credibility and power to blockchain technology and its users as an alternative to the traditional fiat currencies.

Another group of economic analysts believes that all that cryptocurrency needs at the moment is a verified exchange-traded fund (ETF). While an ETF would simplify the process involved in investing in crypto like Bitcoin, the demand for crypto assets must remain constant. I am not given to making predictions because the investment world is full of so many uncertainties. I will rather live with the facts, and in this case, what you need to come to terms with as a newbie investor is that the cryptocurrency will remain volatile for the foreseeable future. As much as you are likely to make huge profits, you are also very likely to lose a sizable portion of your investment, if not all.

Why is Price Stability Important to the Future of Cryptocurrency?

In open markets, price levels are determined by the interplay of supply and demand — when supply and demand rise and fall, so do consumer prices. However, when there are heavy fluctuations in price levels of currencies, there is a serious threat to an economy's financial stability. That is why governments and banks work round the clock to maintain the price stability of their currencies. Imagine a world where all the traditional fiat currencies suddenly disappeared, and everybody around the world had to use cryptocurrencies over the last decade with its dramatic price swings.

It would have been a genuinely chaotic scenario for most individuals and families. At such a time, a father could wake up in the morning and realize that the value of Bitcoin he had in his account that could have paid his daughter's college tuition was no longer worth that much because of a dramatic 6-hour price dip that began because of a tweet from a celebrity or another public figure. How does such a man adjust to that reality under concise notice? The fact is, it would be nearly impossible for anybody to adjust to that kind of reality in such a short time.

If cryptocurrency were the only legal tender globally over the last decade, many people would wake up one morning and be hit with the bitter news that they cannot afford their lifestyle anymore. You might suddenly not be able to pay for the new car you could afford the previous day, and that family vacation you have been planning for months would eventually have to be scrapped all in a moment's breath. When we remove the stability provided by our traditional fiat currencies, the danger of the high volatility of digital currencies becomes more glaring to every one of us. Suddenly, a world where cryptocurrency is the only legal tender does not look so appealing; most of us would not want any part of it.

Now, you have a better understanding of the arguments and concerns raised by some of the critics of cryptocurrency about its widespread adoption across the globe. Most of these critics have cited the high volatility of cryptocurrency as a major drawback for its acceptance, and I agree with that assertion. For cryptocurrencies to become future money, they would have to become much more stable than they are right now. Without the relative stability of top fiat currencies like U.S. dollars, British Pound, and Euros — there would not have been a way for merchants and consumers to determine fair prices for goods and services.

A world where prices of goods and services are changing at every whim would certainly leave the economy in complete disarray. You would not be able to go to the supermarket to get your groceries confidently because of uncertainties about how much the prices of goods might have changed overnight. Even getting a simple cup of coffee from your favorite cafe would become a bit more complex due to price instability. Price stability is crucial to economies because price levels are responsible for inflation and deflation — inflation can be described as an increase in prices with a coinciding fall in the value of a currency. In contrast, deflation is a fall in prices with a coinciding rise in the value of a currency. In other words, when there is a general increase in price levels (typically measured over 12 months), it is called inflation, and when prices fall, it is called deflation.

While some private companies have begun to accept digital currencies as a means of payment, the same energy cannot be expected from countries because the scale of expectations becomes more pronounced. Unlike private companies, when it comes to adopting these coins by countries, things like inflation, deflation, and price stability have to be put into full focus. At the moment, Bitcoin and the other cryptocurrencies are showing nothing close to the level of stability that is required for the sought of widespread acceptance its supporters are muting.

There have been many positives to draw from the decade- long existence of Bitcoin, and with its popularity soaring with each passing day, there is a reason for optimism that someday in the future, cryptocurrency can indeed become the future money.

Ten Important Cryptocurrencies Other Than Bitcoin By Market Capitalization

Bitcoin is one of the most popular cryptocurrencies and an actual standard for other existing ones. It began the trend that welcomed a chain of cryptocurrencies solidified in decentralized peer-to- peer networks. It has amassed a plethora of audiences and still motivates a wide range of followers worldwide. As established, there are other forms of cryptocurrencies or digital currencies aside from Bitcoin, and it will be analyzed in this chapter. However, one must bear in mind that this may not be completely comprehensive since over 4,000 digital currencies exist. A legion of these cryptocurrencies has minimal credibility owing to their low followership and trade volume; some are popular with a committed community of backers and investors.

It is noteworthy that the cryptocurrency market is ever- expanding, leaving more than enough room for the birth of a digital token within a few hours. While Bitcoin holds the number one spot as the pacesetter, some analysts adopt many steps for evaluating tokens other than BTC. It is not uncommon for these analysts to issue a great deal of importance to ranking coins relative to one another regarding market capitalization. This has been considered during the compilation of the top ten list, but keep in mind that there are an array of reasons a digital token will make it into the list.

1. Ethereum (ETH)

The one that tops the list is Ethereum. This Bitcoin alternative is a decentralized software platform that helps in the construction of smart contracts and decentralized applications (dapps) that operates without any glitch, fraud, interference, or control from an outside source or a third party. One fundamental goal behind this digital currency is to create a decentralized body of financial products easily accessible to anybody globally— irrespective of race, ethnicity, or beliefs.

Consequently, this makes the implications for some citizens in some countries more compelling because those without state infrastructures and state identification can be in contact with financial institutions for financial products such as bank loans, bank accounts, insurance, among others. The applications that operate on Ethereum are run on ether, which serves as its platform-specific cryptographic token. This same ether acts as a vehicle that helps one to navigate the Ethereum platform. Most developers and digital experts look for it so that they can develop or run applications inside Ethereum.

However, some investors seek to add more to their chain of cryptocurrencies by purchasing other digital currencies using ether. 2015 was the year that witnessed the birth of ether, and since then, it has risen to be the second-largest digital currency by the standards of market capitalization after Bitcoin. Despite its ranking, it is way behind the dominant cryptocurrency by a significant margin. An analysis made in January 2021 confirmed that ether's market cap is estimated to be around 19% of Bitcoin's size.

A year before the release of ether, Ethereum launched a presale for the digital platform. This move was warmly received, and it attracted an overwhelming response, leaving an avenue to introduce the age of the Initial Coin Offering, otherwise called (ICO). As far as Ethereum is concerned, ICO can be used to "codify, decentralize, secure and trade just about anything." Following the criticism of the decentralized autonomous organization (DAO) in 2016, Ethereum experienced a division— it split into Ethereum (ETH) and Ethereum Classic (ETC).

At the beginning of the year, Ethereum had a market capitalization of $138.3 billion and a per token value of $1,218.59. The plan for 2021 is to usher in a change in its consensus algorithm from proof-of-work to proof-of-stake. This change will make Ethereum's network run itself using far less energy and Improved transaction speed. As its name suggests, proof-of-stake allows the network users to "stake" their ether to the network.

Which in turn offers security to the network and processes the transactions that take place. For the participants, they are rewarded ether, and it is similar to an interesting account. This can be compared to Bitcoin's proof-of-work approach, where miners are awarded more Bitcoin for processing transactions.

2. Litecoin (LTC)

This cryptocurrency came into existence in 2011. The decade-old digital currency was among the few that toed in the path of Bitcoin. Over the years, it has earned the name the "silver to Bitcoin's gold." An MIT graduate and a former Google engineer named Charlie Lee founded Litecoin. Its primary function is to be based on an open-source global payment network free from any form of control by any central authority. It employs what is known as "scrypt" as a proof-of-work, which can be decoded using consumer-grade CPUs.

Even though Litecoin takes its cue from Bitcoin and is similar to the latter in many ways, it has a faster block generation rate, which offers a faster transaction confirmation time. Their market not only gathers an army of developers, as there are a growing number of merchants that accept digital currency. The analysis made in January 2021 shows that Litecoin's market capitalization is about $10.1 billion, with a per token value of $153.88, making it to be the number 6 on the world's largest cryptocurrency chart.

3. Cardano (ADA)

Cardano is a project founded by engineers, mathematicians, and cryptography experts. It was brought to life after a disagreement with some officials in Ethereum. There was disunity in the decisions concerning the steps and directions Ethereum was taking, so Charles Hoskinson, one of Cardano's co-founders who was also one of the founders of Ethereum, worked hand in hand with other like-minds. Their plan was achieved as it introduced Cardano, an "ouroboros proof-of-stake," to the market. The pioneers of this digital currency made its blockchain through extensive experimentation and careful peer-reviewed research.

For the project, a group of researchers penned down more than 90 pages with a long list of different topics on blockchain technology, which became the cornerstone of Cardano. It became one of a kind among its proof-of-stake peers and other large cryptocurrencies following its meticulous process. Although it is still in its early stages, it has been tagged as "Ethereum's Killer," with a blockchain capacity to do more. While it has defeated Ethereum to the proof-of-stake consensus model, it is lagging in decentralized financial applications. One of its goals is to become a global financial operating system by creating decentralized financial products like Ethereum. Another is establishing guaranteed solutions for chain interoperability, legal contract tracing, voter fraud, among other problems. Its market capitalization earlier in the year was $9.8 billion, with one ADA for $0.31.

4. Polkadot (DOT)

This is a cryptocurrency with a distinctive proof-of-stake. Its fundamental goal is to deliver interoperability among other blockchains. It is designed to connect both permissioned and permissionless blockchains and oracles that offer systems the ability to function and work together under one roof. It was designed by Gavin Wood, who happened to be an important member of the board of Ethereum's founders but had a different view on the project's future.

Polkadot's most crucial component is its relay chain that allows more than one network to interoperate. It also gives a chance for parallel blockchains with their native tokens to be used for specific cases. The main difference between Polkadot and Ethereum is that developers can develop their blockchain while also adopting the security that Polkadot's chain already has instead of creating just decentralized applications on the digital currency.

Principally, Ethereum offers developers a chance to create new blockchains, creating their security measures. This could allow the smaller projects to be vulnerable to attacks since a larger blockchain needs plenty of security. In Polkadot, the word used in describing it is "shared security." In January, Polkadot's market capitalization was $11.2 billion, and one DOT went for $12.54.

5. Bitcoin Cash (BCH)

This form of digital currency has an important position in the history of altcoins. It is one of the earliest and has established a groundbreaking record of being the most successful hard forks of the original Bitcoin. As far as the cryptocurrency world is concerned, a fork occurs when questions are raised, debates, arguments, and criticism between the key strategic players— the developers and miners.

However, due to the decentralized nature of digital currencies, some wholesale changes to code controlling the coin at hand are defined as a result of the consensus. The mechanism for this process depends on the type of cryptocurrency. When there is a total disagreement, and the factions don't settle for one decision, the digital currency experiences a division, like Ethereum in 2016. This leaves the original chain to remain true to its original cord, while the new chain starts a new life as a different version of the previous changes to its code.

In 2017, Bitcoin cash came into existence after experiencing one of these splits. It was a debate that led to its establishment. Issues raised during the argument centered on scalability; one of Bitcoin's limitations is the size of blocks limited to one megabyte. Bitcoin cash worked on Bitcoin's shortcomings by raising the size of blocks from one to eight megabytes, bearing in mind that the larger the blocks, the more it can hold more transactions, with an increased transaction speed. That was not all; it introduced other changes like removing "the Segregated Witness" protocol that affects block space. In January, Bitcoin cash had a market capitalization of $8.9 billion, with a value per token of $513.45.

6. Stellar (XLM)

Stellar was created by Jed McCaleb, a co-founder of Ripple Labs; he also developed the Ripple protocol but relinquished his role in Ripple. After such a bold step, he embarked on a new project and became one of the founding members of The Stellar Development Foundation. Stellar offers enterprise solutions by linking different financial institutions to make large transactions through its open blockchain network.

They created a platform that combats the long processes and days it costs banks and investment companies to make enormous transactions. With Stellar, such transactions can happen almost suddenly with no glitches at a very affordable cost. It has positioned itself as a server to enterprise blockchain that facilitates institutional transactions and an open blockchain that anyone can use. It allows an avenue for cross-border transactions among any currencies. Lumens is the name of Stellar's indigenous currency, and one of the requirements to transact on the network is to have the current. At the beginning of the year, its market capitalization was $6.1 billion, with a value of 0.27 per token.

7. Chainlink

Its founders are Sergey Nazarov and Steve Ellis. Chainlink is the most widely accepted decentralized oracle network with the power to seal the gap between smart contracts, synonymous with Ethereum and foreign data outside it. It is a known fact that blockchains are not empowered to connect to foreign applications safely. With Chainlink, the decentralized oracle network bridges the gap for the execution of the contracts based on data that are impossible for Ethereum to connect to.

According to Chainlink's website content, there are an array of use cases outlined for its system. One of which is to observe the water supplies for pollution or illicit siphoning inherent in some cities. There are sensors set up to keep track of the corporate consumption, water tables, and the levels of local bodies of water. The Chainlink oracle network monitors this data and reports it directly into a small contract, which in turn issues flood warnings to cities, executes fines, and alerts firms using an excess of the city's water with the incoming data from the oracle network. The Market capitalization of the network issued in 2021 after analysis from experts was at $8.6 billion, with one LINK valued at $21.53.

8. Binance Coin (BNB)

Based on trading volume, this network is one of the most widely accepted exchanges. Changpeng Zhao is the pioneer of Binance Coin. Binance coin acts as a utility cryptocurrency, with its ability to run as a payment method for the fees generated when trading on the Binance Exchange. The token users can trade at a discount since they employ it as a means of payment. This also creates the platform that Binance's decentralized exchange operates on. It was formerly an ER-20 token that worked on the Ethereum blockchain. After a while, it came up with its main net launch. Binance coin's market capitalization released in January was $6.8 billion, with $44.26 to a value of BNB.

9. Tether (USDT)

Tether holds the record of being the first and most popular of a group of stable coins— these are cryptocurrencies with the goal of tag their market value to a currency or another outside reference point to decrease volatility. It was launched in 2014 via their website; its description reads: "a blockchain-enabled platform designed to facilitate the use of fiat currencies digitally." Tether examined the market and noticed how the digital currencies with the a-list rankings like Bitcoin had suffered the severities of consistent periods of dramatic volatility.

Tether and other stable coins are charged to smooth out price fluctuation to lure customers who may be scared of the digital market. Its price is pegged to the U.S. dollar. The system allows users to make transfers from digital currencies back to U.S. dollars in a shorter period than when converting to normal currency. This medium helps many people make the best use of a blockchain network and other related technologies to purchase, sell or pay in native currencies with reduced volatility and complications associated with digital currencies. At the beginning of the year,

Tether ranked the third-largest cryptocurrency with a market capitalization of $24.4 billion and $1 per token value.

10. Monero (MXR)

Momero offers drama-free transactions as it is a trustful, private and untraceable currency. It was introduced in 2014 and is an open-source cryptocurrency. It did not take long before those in the cryptocurrency market began to gain interest in digital currency. It was a concept that was actualized through donations. Monero is strictly donation-based and community-driven, launched with a primary focus on decentralization and scalability.

The network helps to secure one's privacy through a medium known as "ring signatures." While using this technique, there is a group of cryptographic signatures, at least a real participant. They all appear valid, ensuring that the real one is not isolated. As a result of its unique security mechanisms, it has developed an unpleasant reputation since it has been linked to criminal operations on a global scale. Even though Monero offers a stable for criminal operations and transactions, the privacy settings have also proved useful to dissidents of despotic regimes worldwide without a trace. Its market capitalization in January was $2.8 billion and a per token value of $158.37.

Conclusion

Despite the shortcomings of these cryptocurrencies listed above, it has been ascertained that people worldwide would not mind putting their trading skills to the test, owing to the great figures of the various market capitalization. Neither would there be a discontinuity of the ever-evolving digital currencies.

The cryptocurrency world offers a lot of fun, excitement and I know that I have enjoyed every second of my journey in the crypto space. But, more importantly, I have thoroughly enjoyed pouring my experience and expertise into this book, and I hope that you can gain as much as possible from reading it — as you start your crypto adventure. As I have emphasized from the beginning of this book, technology has significantly impacted our lives since the century.

I would not bet against it making a significant contribution to our financial sector or the kind of money we will be spending in the future. The emergence of companies like Amazon, Uber, Lyft, and other internet-related businesses is valid evidence of what can be achieved when ideas meet innovation. The most significant thing that can be drawn from the success of these businesses is where the world is heading right now. The world is gradually shifting from the conventional way of doing things, whereby a business requires a physical presence before it can operate smoothly.

Today, companies like Uber and Amazon have proved that services can be rendered without customers having to leave the comfort of their homes. And the relative ease by which the general public received these businesses shows that people are genuinely getting ready for the much-talked-about jet age. While we are not close to the jet age in technology, our minds are moving so quickly towards an era that would be characterized by speed. From ultra-fast cars to quick service delivery, there is no limit to the possibilities that exist in the future, given the growth of technology in the last few years.

However, the rope that would tie everything together is new money that would be lighter and faster than the traditional fiat currencies such as the U.S. dollars and the British Pound. Thankfully, we already got that when the first Cryptocurrency, Bitcoin, was launched in 2009. As stated earlier, cryptocurrency is decentralized digital money based on highly complex blockchain technology. It was born due to the public growing disillusioned with the manner the traditional banking institutions were managing their money.

The desire to have more control of their money coupled with the 2008 global financial crisis eventually inspired the invention of what has been described as "future money." Bitcoin and other digital currencies' decentralized nature helps shield them from limiting government financial policies that slow down transaction speed. With the world shifting to a free-flowing cashless economy, the introduction of cryptocurrency has been an inspired move that has gained widespread popularity across the globe.

Since 2009, Bitcoin has enjoyed tremendous success and gained a massive following, which has resulted in an unprecedented increase in its value. Back in April, the value of Bitcoin peaked at an all-time high of $63,000 — inadvertently turning some of its early investors into millionaires. Although the value of the flagship cryptocurrency has since dipped by more than 40%, there is still so much optimism and buzz surrounding the crypto space. While Bitcoin remains the biggest and most popular digital currency, its success over the years has inspired the creation of other cryptocurrencies, which are collectively known as altcoins. Today, more than 5,000 cryptocurrencies are available in the market, but a few of them have garnered strong followership. Some of these cryptocurrencies include Dogecoin, Litecoin, Ethereum, Ripple, Monero, Cardano, Polkadot, Binance coin, etc.

Unsurprisingly, the crypto space has faced heavy criticisms from the traditional banking systems and the governments of countries across the globe, who are wary of the lack of regulation on these coins. Despite the growing popularity of cryptocurrency, it is still not seen as a legal tender and has been chiefly used to complete peer-to-peer transactions through cryptocurrency exchange platforms. However, with more people entering into the crypto space in the last few years due to the tremendous gains made from its more recent price surges — the corporate world has begun to notice the sheer size of the cryptocurrency market.

As a result, many big-name companies have started allowing their customers to make payments for their services using Bitcoin and other digital currencies. Today, Bitcoin, along with other cryptos, can be used to meet basic needs, such as paying for a cup of coffee from your favorite cafe. On the other hand, many people are making tremendous profits from investing in digital currencies as they would in other assets, like stocks, gold, or forex. There is no doubt that cryptocurrency is fast becoming a convenient alternative to traditional fiat currencies from the current trend. However, it is still some way off from achieving the same level of widespread acceptance enjoyed by some of the world's top fiat currencies.

While the decentralized control of cryptocurrency has been its most significant selling point, it also poses the greatest impediment to its mainstream adoption. Most governments are wary of giving cryptocurrency an open field to play because they are limited in regulating all crypto-related activities. In addition, cryptocurrency's strict user anonymity may be popular with its supporters. Still, the function has been abused by criminals and terrorist organizations to perpetrate illegal activities such as drug trafficking and fraud. More importantly, we have seen that cryptocurrency exchange platforms are not immune to attacks from criminally minded hackers.

The case of now-defunct high-profile exchange Mt. Gox, who declared bankruptcy after hackers successfully stole more than $400 million from their platform, is a firm reminder of the risks involved within the cryptocurrency space. However, the most intriguing thing about these thefts is that cryptocurrency's user anonymity means it will be impossible to trace the money or find the perpetrators of the dastardly act.

Interestingly, the glaring security risks associated with cryptocurrency have not stopped the crypto space from expanding rapidly. This can mostly be put down to the massive gains being made by those invested in these coins. However, another thing we have come to associate with cryptocurrency over the years is their enormous price fluctuations. As I pointed out in the book, cryptocurrencies are highly volatile — and their value is primarily determined by how much a buyer is willing to pay at a particular point in time. The last 12 months have been particularly great for cryptocurrencies, as some of the more popular coins enjoyed a remarkable increase in value. For example, the value of Bitcoin steadily rose from mid-March 2020 until it finally peaked at $63,000 in April. Just as we have seen with cryptocurrency over the last decade, the price of Bitcoin suffered a massive dip in its value of more than 40 percent in less than a month.

For analysts, cryptocurrency's massive price swings make it difficult to predict its value at any point in time. Meanwhile, this high volatility could mean hefty profits for those who have invested their hard-earned money in the crypto space. It could also result in the loss of most of their investment or all of it. That is why I have advised potential investors to approach the crypto market with a lot of caution.

Apart from doing an extensive investigation of any crypto exchange platform you are considering putting your money on, you must also endeavor to do adequate research about the type of cryptocurrency you would like to purchase. While I have taken time to draw up a comprehensive list of some of the top cryptocurrencies in the market today, it is never enough to base your financial decisions solely on another person's point of view. Also, I generously shared a story of my personal experience from the past as I tried to find my feet as a newbie investor and business owner. As you venture into the crypto market as a newbie investor, make sure you watch out for the pitfalls I have painstakingly highlighted in various parts of the book.

As a young entrepreneur, I almost let the fear of missing out (FOMO) push me into making a disastrous financial decision that would have probably scarred me for life. I was ready to jump into an unfamiliar field without arming myself with extensive knowledge about everything that pertains to it. I was miraculously rescued from a dicey situation, but life may not be so forgiving next time or to you! And that is what FOMO does to most people — pushes them into making "blind," rushed decisions with possibly grave consequences. As a potential crypto investor, do not be blinded by the low price of a particular cryptocurrency and rush into investing.

What if the price dips further? What if you lose all your investment? There are several cryptocurrencies available in the market — take your time to study as many as you can. There will always be opportunities to make gains in the crypto market, so you do not need to rush into any decision because you are afraid to miss out. Moreover, I advise that you diversify your investment by spreading your money across multiple digital currencies that you have painstakingly researched. On the other hand, you can also diversify your investment portfolio by putting all your money into cryptocurrency and investing in more stable assets like gold or stocks.

There are many risks surrounding Bitcoin and other digital currencies. Still, with the proper guidance and complete commitment to continue educating yourself about the crypto space, you can avoid most of the common mistakes made by newbie investors. The cryptocurrency world is continuously expanding, and new coins are being added to the market faster than you can get a grip on the older ones, so you must keep yourself updated at all times. Finally, I would always advise anyone to invest in Bitcoin because I believe it is the future. I'm not one to give any predictions, but the likes of Bitcoin, Ethereum, Dogecoin, Litecoin, and other top digital currencies have reached a level of popularity. I believe it is much easier for them to be widely accepted globally than for them to fail and go extinct. It is nearly impossible to determine when this wide acceptance would happen. Still, with more countries opening their doors to cryptocurrency, we can be sure of one thing — the crypto craze has begun!

www.ingramcontent.com/pod-product-compliance
Lightning Source LLC
Chambersburg PA
CBHW062110220526
45471CB00010B/3684